AIR FORCE

A Pictorial History of American Airpower

AIR FORCE

A Pictorial History of American Airpower

By MARTIN CAIDIN

In cooperation with the U. S. Air Force

BRAMHALL HOUSE · NEW YORK

for
Colonel "Chuck" Whitehead, USAF

This edition is published by Bramhall
House, a division of Clarkson N. Potter, Inc.,
by arrangement with Holt, Rinehart & Winston, Inc.

(B)

© 1957 by Martin Caidin
Printed in the United States of America
Layout by the author
Typography by Edwin H. Kaplin
Library of Congress Catalog Card Number: 57-6575

Foreword

AIR FORCE is a pictorial documentation of fifty years of the development of airpower within the United States Air Force and its preceding organizations. It is not a book about airplanes, or even about airplanes within the Air Force. We have presented here only those airplanes which made definite and vital contributions to the development of airpower, either through their application in war or as vehicles used in peacetime to develop the techniques of air combat and to further a broader understanding of the proper use of the aerial weapon.

The reader will find many historical photographs which are reproduced here for the first time. Indeed, we have been unusually fortunate in being able to demonstrate pictorially, for example, that virtually every method of bombing attack employed by the AAF in World War II had been practiced and developed before that war started.

We have attempted to demonstrate the development and the use of the airplane through the years not merely as a shooting and a bombing platform, but as a *weapons system*. Many of the photographs herein are not of airplanes, but of the men who flew them, of the many branches of the vast logistical army which enabled the weapons to be used. Airpower is a handmaiden to the man on the ground; it has always been so, and so it will alway be.

The writer personally searched through every single file in the vast USAF storage facility in the Pentagon. The historical files of the Institute of Aeronautical Sciences were generously made available to the author. Headquarters, USAF, requested its field organizations to participate in the enormous research project which went into the making of AIR FORCE, and field OIS personnel performed a yeoman's job in forwarding material for consideration in this book. Several private collections of historical photographs were opened for research, and the voluminous files of the major aircraft companies were examined for additional material.

The contents of the book were studied in joint and lengthy conferences by members of the Historical Division, Air University, USAF, by members of air staff and policy divisions, Headquarters, USAF. Official records and documents which have never been seen by the public eye were plumbed to assure that AIR FORCE would be the most authentic book possible on this subject.

It would be difficult to list here all those persons and institutions whose contributions and long hours of effort made this book possible. The author wishes, however, to thank particularly Lt. Colonel Gordon C. Furbish, Chief, Still Picture Section, Office of Information Services, for "bird-dogging" much of the research effort. No two people worked harder than Mrs. Margaret Abendschein and Mrs. B. L. Hardesty, PRSD, USAF, to complete the Pentagon research work; their efforts were aided in no small degree by Mr. Joseph L. Albright. Elizabeth Brown of the I. A. S. was more than generous in researching thousands of pictures for historical material, and special thanks are due to Peter M. Bowers for his World War I research effort. Captain James Sunderman, of the USAF Magazine and Book Branch, performed invaluable service in attending to many research problems, and I am particularly grateful for his assistance. Special thanks are due to Major Raymond E. Houseman, who has worked with the writer for many years in accumulating data and photographic material; to Major Keith M. Garrison, who proved particularly adept at ferreting out rare material; and, Captain Carl B. McCamish, who provided the writer with invaluable research material not available in any other form. A personal vote of thanks goes to Stewart Richardson; and, above all, to my editor, Robert D. Loomis, who was of enormous personal and professional assistance through every stage of the project.

MARTIN CAIDIN

Contents

HIGH FLIGHT

Pilot Officer John G. Magee, Jr.

Oh! I have slipped the surly bonds of earth

And danced the skies on laughter-silvered wings;

Sunward I've climbed, and joined the tumbling mirth

Of sun-split clouds — and done a hundred things

You have not dreamed of — wheeled and soared and swung

High in the sunlit silence. Hov'ring there

I've chased the shouting wind along, and flung

My eager craft through footless halls of air.

Up, up the long, delirious, burning blue

I've topped the wind-swept heights with easy grace

Where never lark, nor even eagle flew —

And, while with silent lifting mind I've trod

The high untrespassed sanctity of space

Put out my hand and touched the face of God.

THE BEGINNING

Quick death in the air and a preference for horses

Early in 1907 the organization which was to become the most powerful military force in history suffered the sudden loss of fully half of its enlisted strength. Outraged at Army discipline, a private fled to the hills, leaving behind him a lonely corporal as the sole enlisted man in the United States' fledgling air force.

Actually, the private's unexpected defection mattered little. For in the early summer of 1909 the nation's new air service did not yet have its first airplane *(above)*. It lacked equipment or doctrine, existed on funds scrimped from wire-laying appropriations, and was hard pressed to find any specific duties for its one officer to perform.

The beginning of our modern air force could hardly have been less auspicious. On August 1, 1907, the United States Army yielded to insistence that it extend its study of military operations to the air, and grudgingly established within the Signal Corps an Aeronautical Division which was charged with "all matters pertaining to military ballooning, air machines, and all kindred subjects."

It would be pleasant to record that this date, so momentous in retrospect, marked the beginning of a major effort to place the United States in a commanding position with respect to airpower. The unhappy truth is that any such statement would be pure myth.

By the close of 1904, Orville and Wilbur Wright were entertaining inquiries from foreign governments for the purchase of their airplanes. These bids the brothers held in abeyance, believing that their own country should be the first to profit by their years of labor. Unfortunately, the letters they dispatched to the Army authorities, listing their accomplishments and requesting permission to demonstrate their machines, were answered by abstract form replies which stated that the Army's Board of Ordnance and Fortification did not grant financial assistance to inventors. Faced with these inexplicable communications, the Wrights, who had requested not one penny of subsidy, promptly turned to other sources.

In fairness, one must admit that the hapless members of the Board of Ordnance and Fortification were not entirely unjustified in adopting a skeptical attitude toward the Wrights' claims. Early in 1898, when the streets of Washington resounded with militant speeches against Spain's maltreatment of Cuba, the potential advantages of air machines to be used against the Spaniards appealed highly to the Army and Navy. They established a joint board to investigate the merits of Professor Samuel Langley's steam-powered aerodrome, and bestowed upon the professor a handsome subsidy in the amount of $50,000.

On October 7, 1903, Langley attempted his first launching from a houseboat on the Potomac River near Widewater, Virginia. Moments later the professor stared in horror as five years of his life plunged awkwardly into the river. One month later he tried again, only to reap the bitter reward of listening to his pilot's curses as he was being fished from the water.

This second failure and its attendant criticism caused the Army to release its official report of January 6, 1904, which stated that ". . . the claim that an engine-driven, man-carrying aerodrome has been constructed lacks the proof which actual flight alone can give."

Thus the inquiries of the Wrights in 1904 and 1905

arrived at precisely the time when the Army Board still smarted under a storm of Congressional and newspaper ridicule for its "asinine expenditure" of government funds. Nothing can be more unfair to the career officer than public chastisement for committing an honest error. Small wonder that these officers dismissed the Wrights with a form letter which rejected commitment to any further folly with air machines.

There were in Washington, however, influential officials who could envision, though dimly, a proper role for the airplane in our military establishment. Their insistence that the United States needed military aircraft bore fruit in President Theodore Roosevelt's officially expressed desire to have the matter investigated; soon thereafter the Board of Ordnance and Fortification extended to the Wright Brothers an invitation personally to state their case for their flying machine.

This, then, was the tortuous route which finally caused the Signal Corps on December 23, 1907, to release to the public its Specification No. 486, calling for bids on the delivery of an air machine which could fly faster than forty miles an hour, which could remain aloft for at least one hour with a crew of two, and probably the most onerous requirement of all, that it be able of transport in a four-wheeled, mule-driven wagon.

Of the forty-one bids received, that of the Wrights appeared the most promising, and on February 10, 1908,

The crumpled wreckage of the Wright airplane at Fort Meyer in September, 1908. The airplane was making turns at a height of 150 feet when a propeller snagged a rudder brace wire. Out of control, the machine plunged earthward. The crash hurled Orville

Wright clear, but Lt. Thomas E. Selfridge was pinned beneath the wreckage. Several hours later the young officer died, the first air fatality in our military air history. Wright suffered serious injuries, but returned the next year to deliver to the Army its first airplane.

The new Wright Model B airplane, which featured wheels and skids, and eliminated the need for the bulky and dangerous launching platform and rails. With its new undercarriage, the Model B could land and take off from open fields, doing away with the need for a "launching crew." In 1911, a Wright Model B flew with two men 106 miles nonstop from Laredo to Eagle Pass, Texas in 2 hours and 10 minutes. Less successful was the return flight; engine trouble forced the plane down in four feet of water in the Rio Grande.

A blistering 42.583 mph

the Army signed a contract with the brothers for its first airplane. Initial flight tests began at Fort Myer, Virginia, on September 3rd, when Orville Wright managed to remain aloft for one minute and eleven seconds.

Two weeks later disaster struck. Orville was making routine turns at a height of 150 feet, carrying with him Lieutenant Thomas E. Selfridge as a passenger. Suddenly a propeller struck a rudder brace wire. Before the horrified spectators, the airplane plunged to the ground, hurling Orville Wright clear, but pinning Selfridge beneath the wreckage. Several hours later Selfridge was dead, the first air fatality in American heavier-than-air military history. Suffering from a fractured thigh and broken ribs, Orville languished in a hospital for seven weeks. The Army reluctantly postponed its acceptance tests until the following summer.

On June 20, 1909, the Wrights returned with a rebuilt and improved machine, and spent the next five weeks carefully grooming their airplane for its military trials. On July 27th, Orville Wright flew with Lieutenant Frank P. Lahm for 1 hour, 12 minutes and 40 seconds, fulfilling the requirement of remaining aloft for at least one hour with a passenger. Three days later, flying in view of more than seven thousand persons who spurred him on with thundering cheers, Orville Wright sped over five miles of broken country on a two-way course to average a blistering 42.583 miles per hour. The airplane had passed all its tests — including that of transport in the mule-driven wagon — and on August 2, 1909, the Army proudly accepted its first flying machine.

The ragged stepchild

The new Aeronautical Division made little impression upon the 1907 Congress, which demonstrated its skepticism toward military aviation by refusing with hardly a murmur of dissent a half-million dollar request for aeronautics in the fiscal year 1908. Fortunately for those officers possessed of the urge to fly, the Army's contract with the Wrights called for the training of two

Orville Wright is shown at the controls of the Wright airplane at Fort Meyer, on September 12, 1908. Shortly after this picture was taken, he took off and remained airborne with Lieutenant Frank P. Lahm as a passenger for 1 hour and 12 minutes. Three days later Orville Wright sped over five miles of broken country on a two-way course to hit a new record of 42.583 miles per hour. Seven thousand persons cheered the flight, were on hand to witness the two Wrights' demonstrations of their machine to Army authorities.

One of the rare Burgess-Wright tractors on the Army airfield at Texas City, Texas, in 1913. A marked advance over the more fragile pusher airplanes with their exposed wing seats, the Burgess was used for reconnaissance flights in 1913 over the Texas-Mexico border. This particular airplane is the Signal Corps' first Burgess, and its nineteenth aircraft, assigned to the 1st Aero Squadron. Lt. William C. Sherman is seated in front, Lt. Thomas DeW. Milling is in the rear cockpit.

officers in the "handling and operation of this flying machine." In early October, 1909, the Army transferred its sole airplane to College Park, Maryland, and hopefully dispatched Lieutenants Frank P. Lahm and Frederic E. Humphreys to win their wings. On October 26th, Wilbur Wright stood on the ground and proudly watched his two students circle College Park as the Army's first aviators.

Shortly afterward Wright and the two new pilots took up for three hours of unofficial flight instruction Lieutenant B. D. Foulois, recently returned from overseas duty. It was indeed fortunate that they did so, for soon Foulois found himself the only man in the Aeronautical Division with any flying experience. The Army had unceremoniously ordered Lahm back to his horses in the Cavalry, and returned Humphreys to the Engineers.

Winter cold and high winds made continued flying at College Park a hazardous affair with an already hazardous airplane, and in February, 1910, the airplane arrived at the Fort Sam Houston drill field near San Antonio, Texas. Lieutenant Foulois, despite his casual experience, set out to teach himself to solo; on March 2nd his memorable achievement of staggering into the air and returning to the ground unharmed after seven and a half minutes afforded the Aeronautical Division a shaky continued lease on life.

The state of affairs of the nation's air arm in 1910 can best be appreciated by the fact that during the next seven months Foulois accumulated only nine hours in the air. The Signal Corps had allowed him no more than $150 to operate his airplane; had not Foulois supplemented this niggardly pittance with personal funds, the

A Wright Type C trainer with pontoons (right) replacing the wheels and skids normally used, shown at Pasay Manila Bay, in July, 1913. Flown by the Aviation Detachment in the islands, it was used as a training airplane for four officers and one enlisted man.

The Aeronautical Division's eighth airplane was this Curtiss tricycle gear model, mounting a pusher engine (below). With the Wright airplanes, it was used for training flights at College Park, Maryland. Walking toward the camera is Lt. Lewis H. Brereton.

The first Army airplane in the Philippines, at Fort McKinley, in March, 1912. Standing by the engine is Lieutenant Frank P. Lahm, who used the airplane both to demonstrate its possible military value, and to train other men. Flying in the Philippines could be perilous; pilots seated on the wings were exposed to locust swarms which smashed into their faces, forcing a hasty retreat to the ground.

Wright machine would have moldered on the dirt floor of its ramshackle shed.

By the spring of 1911 the Army's one airplane had become too dilapidated to permit further safe flight. The Army's minor flying activity might have ended altogether had not a patriotic American, Robert F. Collier, generously loaned his privately owned Wright B airplane to the Signal Corps until such time as government funds should become available to buy a new machine. On March 3rd the new Wright B demonstrated to the Army for the first time the possible military use of the airplane. Foulois and P. O. Parmelee (killed the following year) of the Wright Company flew 106 miles along the Texas-Mexico border from Laredo to Eagle Pass in two hours and ten minutes. Less successful was their return flight on March 7th to Fort McIntosh, where they created a re-

sounding splash in four feet of water in the Rio Grande. This occurrence proved the wisdom of the Army's requirement that the airplane be transportable in a wagon, for the wrecked Wright B completed its journey to the fort in precisely this fashion.

On the same day that Foulois and Parmelee fluttered their way to Eagle Pass, Congress voted $125,000 specifically for the Signal Corps' ragged stepchild, which at once ordered three Wright and two Curtiss airplanes. With its new machines the Aeronautical Division emerged from the one-pilot, one-airplane apathy in which it had been kept for two years.

Increased flying in the primitive machines made it inevitable that misfortune should descend upon the group. Their airplanes had no cockpits; the men sat precariously balanced on the leading edge of a wing, exposed

In November, 1912, the Signal Corps tested air-to-ground wireless communications for artillery spotting at Fort Riley, Kansas.

Four officers who participated in radio tests were *(left to right)* Lt. H. H. Arnold; Col. E. A. Millar; Lts. Mauborgne and DeRussy Hoyle.

to the slipstream. They had no flying clothes, but struggled into whatever gear would most effectively protect their bodies. Their machines were incredibly fragile, and by today's standards the Wright control system was appallingly difficult to master. Death was a constant companion in the air, abetted by mechanics who were forced to learn their trade by the simple expedient of trial and error.

During flight training in Texas, Lieutenant John C. Walker so narrowly escaped death that he refused ever to fly again. Lieutenant Paul A. Beck plunged two hundred feet and staggered away miraculously unhurt from a mass of wreckage. And on May 10, 1911, Lieutenant G. E. M. Kelly smashed into the ground with such impact that he was pitched forward one hundred feet and died later of a fractured skull. His death so upset the local Army commander that he forbade any further flying from *his* drill field.

Plans were under way, however, to renew training at the original College Park Field in Maryland. Several men assigned to duty, including Lieutenants Henry H. Arnold and Thomas DeW. Milling, had received their initial instruction from the Wright Company. Other pilots "graduated" from College Park during the spring and

Captain Charles DeF. Chandler and Lieutenant Roy T. Kirtland pose in the Wright B airplane with a Lewis machine gun; air tests were held in 1912 with this rapid-fire weapon for the first time, provoking much speculation about its use against masses of infantry.

summer of 1911; compared to the doldrums of 1910 and early 1911, the fledgling air force was running in high gear.

The restrictions of winter flying, as well as the Signal Corps' desire to gain experience with its new machines in various geographical locations, caused the opening of new training schools and the transfer of airplanes to overseas stations. In November, 1911, the Aeronautical Division loaded its airplanes, horses, mules, equipment, ground crews and pilots into a special train and packed them off to the Barnes Farm in Augusta, Georgia, to open a new flying school. The anticipated excellent flying weather of the Southern state vanished before a wild snowstorm which blanketed the field. Soon after the unwelcome snow melted, heavy floods inundated the area. The men hastily evacuated the more valuable horses and mules and placed the airplanes on high scaffolds to protect them from the rising streams. Obviously the art of flying was going to encounter greater difficulties than anyone had expected.

The lean years between 1910 and 1914 were a critical period for the new air arm. Meager funds, primitive equipment and antique airplanes virtually restricted the Army's aviators to the basic hazards of getting off the ground and returning alive to earth. There did not exist at this time even a suggestion of tactical doctrine. Commanding officers snorted at airplanes as ridiculous contraptions which might eventually prove of some minor use for reconnaissance. Reflecting the nation's attitude toward its military stepchild, the Congress appropriated the insignificant sum of $350,000 for military aeronautics — and flying officers choked on their own rage as they read of expenditures by Germany for the same period of $28,000,000!

It was fortunate for our country that the military aviators of these trying days did not hesitate to experiment with their ideas — concepts too often looked upon with disfavor by their superiors. Between 1910 and 1914 the small group of military air pioneers conducted tests which showed to a few visionaries the course of future development the military airplane might follow.

Early in 1910 and in 1911, Lieutenant Paul Beck made crude attempts to drop "bombs" from aircraft. In October of that year Riley E. Scott tested the first American bombsight and bomb-dropping device, accurate enough to dump small 15-lb. missiles within ten feet of a small target from a 400-ft. altitude.

The first rifle-firing from an aircraft in this country occurred on August 20, 1910. Lieutenant Jacob E. Fickel of the 29th Infantry flew with Glenn H. Curtiss at the old Sheepshead Bay Race Track near New York City; he put two bullets into a small target from an altitude of 100 feet. This initial gunnery attempt proved little except that a gun could be fired from an airplane; it did, however, lead directly to research for aerial gunsights.

In June, 1912, Captain Charles DeF. Chandler and Lieutenant Milling fired a Lewis machine gun from an airplane, causing much speculation on the effect of rapid-fire airborne weapons against ground troops. Fliers leaned far over the wings of their fragile machines to take aerial photographs, and on several occasions they demonstrated the advantages of two-way radio telegraphy between their airplanes and the ground. At Fort Riley, Kansas, in 1912, Lieutenants Arnold and Bradley in a Wright C spotted artillery fire for ground troops. The same year the Army sent its planes to participate in maneuvers near New York.

Flying training began in the Philippine Islands in 1912 with the arrival at Fort William McKinley near Manila of one Wright B airplane. During 1912 and 1913, Lieutenant Lahm instructed four officers and one enlisted man; the second year he received a Wright C trainer, which was modified with pontoons for water take-offs and landings. Flying at this outpost meant overcoming obstacles not usually encountered in the States, and agitated pilots were at times forced to dive for the ground when dense swarms of locusts smashed into their faces.

Early in 1913, the Signal Corps activated the 1st

Hanging desperately to the wing of this Curtiss pusher, Lieutenant J. E. Fickel of the 29th Infantry flew with Glenn H. Curtiss at the old Sheepshead Bay Race Track near New York City, on August 20, 1910, to become the first man to fire a rifle from an airplane in flight. Fickel managed to place two bullets into a small target from an altitude of 100 feet, disproving dire warnings that the rifle's recoil would break up the flimsy airplane. The tests at Sheepshead Bay had virtually no direct military value, but they proved to be the experiments which started several companies on efforts to develop rifle and machine-gun sights which would compensate for the height and movement of the airplane when firing at ground targets.

Locusts smashed into their faces...

Aero Squadron at Texas City; until mid-June they flew their nine airplanes with the 2nd Division guarding the Texas border. Operating under the worst of semi-desert conditions, they nevertheless made many flights over wild country and gained invaluable experience in aerial reconnaissance, in the process reducing their airplanes to flying pieces of junk.

By December, 1913, the Army's safety and operational record left much to be desired. Of twenty-four airplanes purchased in four years, nine had been destroyed, and pilots who flew the remaining antiques daily courted suicide. Eleven officers and one enlisted man had been killed, leaving the Aeronautical Division after more than six years with only twelve pilots.

In 1914 the Army concentrated its training at North Island near San Diego, sharing a grass field with Glenn H. Curtiss. The new year was barely six weeks old when additional crashes (including another fatality) and two requested transfers from men who no longer wished to parry with the Grim Reaper focused attention on the sordid safety record. An Army investigating board recommended the immediate condemnation of the eleven existing Curtiss and Wright pusher airplanes. They stalled easily, were flimsy and unreliable, and it was considered little less than miraculous that the eleven airplanes had managed to survive until 1914.

Their condemnation illuminated the sorry mess into which American military aviation had descended. There were left in the Signal Corps but five airplanes, one of which had to be torn down and rebuilt. While this project dragged, military flying was seriously hampered — even as war loomed in Europe and the combatants readied fleets of hundreds of planes for battle.

With few airplanes capable of flight, the Signal Corps turned in desperation to Glenn L. Martin, an in-

This 1917 Wright-Martin scout, replete with motorbike lashed to fuselage *(above)*, was serious Army conception of a military plane; required more practice at untying knots than it did in air skill. In 1911, Lt. Riley E. Scott *(below)* demonstrated bomb-dropping with new device he invented. Bombs were slung in canvas straps, were surprisingly accurate despite the crude equipment used.

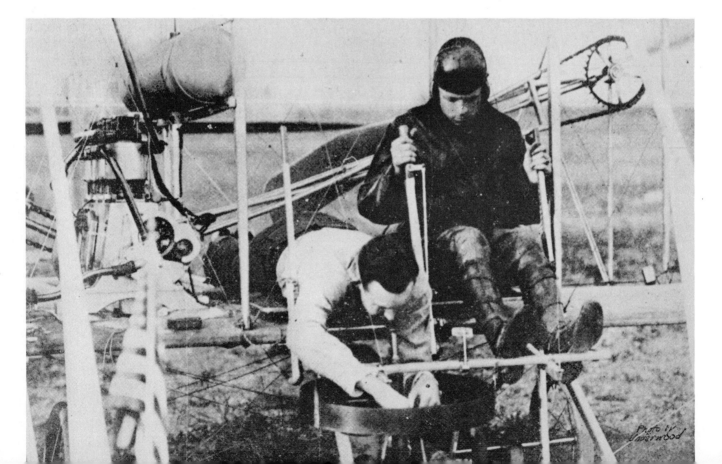

Maintenance in early days could be fatal; mechanics learned their trade by trial and error. This is the Army's 1st Aero Repair Shop, located in 1914 at North Field, San Diego.

dependent designer who had just completed his own sportplane in a Los Angeles workshop. Purchased by the Army and hurriedly converted into a dual trainer, the machine proved successful and paved the way for a new series of Army aircraft supplied by several companies, including Martin.

One thirsty cavalry column

On March 9, 1916, the Mexican bandit, Villa, led his men out of Columbus, New Mexico, leaving behind him seventeen American corpses. An enraged United States government ordered General John J. Pershing to lead an expedition across the Mexican border to bring back Villa, either protesting or bullet-punctured. Thus was provided a splendid opportunity to prove in practice the theories of aerial operations which had been preached with such fervor by the military aviators.

On March 19th and 20th the Army transferred the 1st Aero Squadron from Columbus to Casas Grandes in Mexico. No other action was to prove so conclusively the appalling ineffectiveness of the American air service, for the Squadron's eight Curtiss JN-2 airplanes proved unable even to reach Casas Grandes on their first attempt. Engine trouble forced one airplane to return to its Columbus airfield. Three became lost and wandered helplessly over the desolate Mexican countryside; two of these landed successfully and the third cracked up. The remaining four, clinging grimly together as evening fell, barely managed to make safe emergency landings.

For the next six weeks the crews struggled to perform their duties of reconnaissance, of flying mail and dispatches, and of transporting senior officers about the wild country. The task proved too demanding for the training airplanes, which lacked the power to fly over the mountains of northern Mexico. More than once pilots turned back because they could not cross the peaks, or barely staggered over 10,000-foot ridges with jagged rock looming below their wheels. A thundering downpour once dumped nearly a foot of water into the cockpit of a Curtiss flown by Foulois; moments later his flooded engine choked to a stop. He was able to walk away from a forced landing and returned to his field after a five-hour ride via the dependable horse-drawn wagon.

After six weeks the airplanes were worn out and ragged. Two had crashed. Four others were so in need of parts they were unflyable, and for weeks afterward crewmen and pilots suffered blisters from having to carve new propellers out of logs. On April 20th, five weeks after they entered Mexico, the Army retired its unflyable airplanes from the field. Their total military accomplishment could be summed up in one successful scouting mission: they had once found a lost and thirsty cavalry column.

After ten years —
Disagreement: Dissatisfaction: Weakness

Pershing's Mexican expedition proved conclusively the United States' woeful unpreparedness for any measure of combat aviation. The lonely cries of the few flying officers who besought their superiors and the members of Congress for funds for new equipment and better airplanes served only to irritate these lofty officials.

For its part, the high brass found the aviators too outspoken and too indifferent toward old and established conventional military customs. As early as February, 1916, Brigadier General George P. Scriven protested in

Carrying their entire armament — a .45 Colt pistol for each man — Lts. Edgar S. Gorrell *(left)* and Herbert A. Dargue stand before their Curtiss training airplane at Casas Grandes, Mexico, in 1916. Never designed to fight a war, especially in the mountainous wastes of Mexico, the Curtiss planes proved underpowered and lacking the performance to remain in the air. High mountains often forced pilots to abandon missions, and on one occasion a sudden cloudburst deposited twelve inches of water in the cockpit of one startled pilot; he operated his foot controls entirely under water. The plane's engine died; the pilot managed an emergency landing, and finished his journey by a wagon.

Flooded cockpits and enraged senior officers

damning terms that behind the "unmilitary, insubordinate, and disloyal acts" was a burning ambition to set up a new and independent organization for aviation.

Unhappily for all, the acrimonious debates between ground officers and the impatient aviators served no fruitful purpose. American airpower was at that time no more than a misty wish; consequently, these differences of opinion remained speculative rather than factual.

The sum total of our first ten years of military aviation was voiced by a veteran infantry officer who admitted that "... airplanes could go higher and faster than horses."

This, then, was our pitiful air legacy as we entered into World War I.

A rare documentary picture shows these old Curtiss biplanes in a large group formation (above). This is the type of airplane used during the Mexican expedition; its unsuitability was no reflection on the design, intended only for student training — not military operations under semi-desert conditions of northern Mexico. During W. W. I, Curtiss was most widely used plane in U.S.

A pilot and his observer load mailbags into a Curtiss R training plane (right), which was used during Punitive Expedition for Army support missions. This particular flight was made from Columbus, New Mexico, to Dublan in Mexico. Pilots often smashed propellers in landing on fields; had to carve new props from logs. This pilot wanted no blisters; note spare prop lashed to fuselage.

WAR IN THE AIR

Our pilots flew combat with old planes discarded by French fliers

Between 1909 and April 6, 1917, when Congress declared war on the Central Powers, a total of about 300 airplanes had been purchased by the United States Army. With a sharp eye for posterity a French air officer labeled this motley collection of flying machines *"a magnificent retrospective museum."* The innuendo was fully justified, for not one of these airplanes was fit for combat, and the majority had either crashed or degenerated into uselessness. Indeed, on the day that the United States committed itself to mortal combat in Europe, there were only 55 airplanes in the Army's Aviation Section which could be coaxed into the air. Only *four* machines were considered so modern as to be merely obsolescent, while the others were no more than ragged antiques. The total absence of United States air-combat strength was paralleled by a lack of experienced pilots; among the 1,000 enlisted men and 131 officers of the Aviation Section there was not a single flier who would not be courting suicide in exposing himself to enemy guns.

More distressing than the Army's material deficiency was the shortsightedness of its General Staff. After 32 months of war in Europe and the employment on that battlefield of many thousands of combat airplanes, this distinguished body still ignored our own military aviation requirements and, instead, complained bitterly about disrespectful air officers who flaunted regulations by not wearing cavalry spurs in flight.

The greatest and the most exciting air developments in World War I took place in pursuit, and the cocky little single-seat fighter plane became the chief focus and the symbol of airpower. No other activity in the air enjoyed the attention or the popularity afforded to the agile planes of wood and fabric which spun like whirling dervishes over the front lines. Pilots climbed into glove-tight planes which could explode into balls of fire under the impact of a single well-placed enemy bullet. They flew without parachutes, and their only protection in the air was provided by stove lids which were sometimes bolted behind the seats as armor plating.

American pilots who flew with the British, in the Lafayette Escadrille with the French, or with our own Air Service units proved they had the skill and the daring to become aces. Men like Rickenbacker, Luke, Lufberry, Vaughn, Springs, Kindley, Landis, Swaab and Hunter ran up many air kills in the short time they were able to serve with American units. Their greatest praise came

By the war's end, every American squadron had pilots killed in mid-air disintegrations of these structurally weak French Nieuports.

13

German fighters like this Fokker D-7 (*above*) excelled all others in maneuverability and in climb. The Germans originated the fixed, synchronized machine gun, established the patterns of air combat in formation tactics, and produced the finest and most efficient fighters of the war. Despite the ground victory gained, neither side "won" or "lost" the four-year-old battle in the skies.

The French-designed Spad which went into action near the end of the war was the best plane produced by the Allies. It featured excellent speed and unexcelled diving ability. For some mysterious reason which has never been explained, the U.S. cancelled orders for 3,000 Spads to be built in this country. The Army used Spads after the war, as well as German Fokkers. This picture was taken in the United States in 1923.

An English Bristol fighter on patrol over the Western Front. American industry failed to produce one acceptable fighter plane in time for combat in Europe. Contracts for 2,000 English-designed Bristol fighters were canceled at a cost of $30,000,000 when the first 24 airplanes were found to be structurally inferior, and suicide ships. Justice Charles Evan Hughes damned the U.S. air industry, regretted that "the provisions of the criminal statutes do not reach inefficiency."

U.S. failed to produce one combat-worthy plane

from bewildered German fliers who reported that the Americans fought like "crazy Indians."

The United States had little to do with originating or developing pursuit doctrine during World War I. Congressional promises in 1917 to send a flood of fighting airplanes to Europe proved to be so much political wagging of the jaw. The first American pursuit unit to go into action, flying Nieuport 28s, was the 94th Pursuit Squadron, Captain Eddie Rickenbacker's famous "Hat-in-the-Ring" outfit. Since the 94th did not enter active combat operations until April 14, 1918, it may be seen that the total American unit experience amounted to something less than seven months when it was cut short by the armistice. For the most part, our pilots had no choice but to adopt the tactics which our Allies had developed during their air battles with the Germans.

By July, 1917, mass-pursuit action had become common on both sides. Baron Manfred von Richthofen was leading his famed *Jagdstaffel* against large units of Allied fighters. The forces involved in these swirling jousts comprised twenty to forty planes; the era of the individual pilot, the daredevil ace who fought alone, was ended. The American fighter pilots who arrived in Europe dutifully heeded the lessons of their more experienced Allies and followed suit in combat.

World War I gave rise to a concept which has well withstood the test of time — the all-important value of the outstanding fighter pilot. It soon became obvious in battle that the leading killers of the air all shared one outstanding trait: *eagerness to fight*. These were the elite, gifted with the greatest energy and resourcefulness and the sound judgment required to temper their offensive spirit. Fighting was the most important factor in life. The record confirms the indispensability of this eagerness to pursue and kill; some 200 pilots on both sides destroyed the great majority of all planes shot down during the entire war.

On July 24, 1917, Congress made a grandiose gesture to overcome the results of its indifference to and its neglect of aviation by appropriating $640,000,000 to build up our air strength. Along with its verbal assaults on the sensibilities of the people, Congress anticipated that this monetary redemption of its own inadequacies would overnight place the United States in a commanding position in the air. Nothing could have been less realistic.

The massive appropriation bore temporary fruit in the form of thousands of young aspirants who stormed flying schools the nation over. The Curtiss company rushed hundreds of Jenny trainers from its factories, and with a great carnival atmosphere the training program

A Curtiss flying boat passes over the USS *New York*. By the end of the war, the Navy had 500 planes of various types, many of which were flying in Europe. Admiral William S. Sims claimed that the Navy's air arm was "a factor in persuading the enemy to ac- knowledge defeat." General Pershing disagreed, said Navy's planes "possessed no advantages over destroyers, and (their) use was certainly of no immediate aid in meeting the crisis that confronted us on the Western Front . . . the most important consideration."

Originally designed as a two-seat fighter, the U.S.-built DH-4 (above) was heavy and clumsy, flew like an overloaded truck. Poor design made the airplane a "flaming coffin," to distress of our pilots. Most DH-4s sent to France had to be torn down and rebuilt.

The tremendous size of the Zeppelin Giant R-7 (below) is evident in comparison with the size of the people in the crowd inspecting the German bomber. American industry had nothing to compare with this tremendous German-built bombing machine.

View from the air: preview of another war

spat out its hundreds of pilots. No one seemed to notice that while these men could fly, they did not know how to *fight,* nor had they ever fired a weapon in the air.

By December, 1917, the United States had shipped 1,800 honor graduates of ground schools to France to receive their flying instruction in that country. The training plans in France disintegrated completely, and many of the honor students were confined to overcrowded mobilization camps where they were mistreated by officers who regarded them as draft dodgers deserving only the strictest discipline. Colonel Hiram Bingham reported that they were the unhappy victims of "serious and exasperating delays, disappointments and 'raw deals.' " It was, as Bingham sadly concluded, "the worst page in the history of the Air Service."

By May, 1918, the situation had degenerated into almost total chaos. Many of the 30,000 men who were in France, England and Italy despaired of ever receiving their promised airplanes. The Air Historian, Lt. Colonel H. A. Toulmin, Jr., reported that the Air Service program was "a practical failure; was facing the possibilities of disaster . . . and was faced with moral and mental disintegration and disarrangement, which was insidiously

wrecking the very integrity and the morale of the entire service."

Well aware that American production might not be able to meet the demands made upon it, General Pershing had contracted with the French and Italian governments for the delivery of 6,000 new planes and 12,000 engines before June, 1918. But even this came to nothing, for the Aircraft Production Board failed to meet its obligations to send promised tools and other materials, causing these nations to cancel their contracts.

It was this failure which forced the United States to purchase, as Pershing noted bitterly, "inferior types of planes from the French." Our pilots flew old Nieuports which French fliers had discarded; many an American pilot discovered to his horror that his Nieuport had shed the fabric from its wings, causing the airplane to disintegrate in mid-air. Before the armistice was signed, every single American squadron at the front saw men die because of their defective Nieuport fighters.

The resounding huzzahs which greeted the British-designed and American-built DH-4 were a marvel of propagandist buffoonery. Those machines which reached France were so inferior in workmanship and defective

A French-built Salmson observation plane of the Army's 1st Aero Squadron flies toward enemy on a patrol flight. French-built Breguets, U.S. DH-4s, were AEF bombers.

Incredible devastation wrought by massed artillery fire is dramatically illustrated in this rare photograph *(above)*. The slow and cumbersome observation planes used by both sides over the Western Front proved valuable for directing the fire of artillery weapons; aerial photographs for the first time allowed an over-all conception of ground situation, permitted better evaluation of damage suffered by enemy in concentrated barrages.

Water geysers mark the explosions *(right)* of four bombs which struck as near misses and direct hits against the Chickaldene Bridge at Ardan. There were few occasions when planes made serious attempts to help isolate the battle front from enemy's sources of supply. Not until the last months of the war were there constant air attacks by fighters and bombers on a mass scale, which were designed to assist our troops in the field by cutting the enemy rail lines and roads.

In a rare picture of war above the clouds, a British two-seat fighter *(above)* pursues a fleeing German observation plane. Early in the war pilots attacked one another with rocks, pistols.

Ungainly, fragile and underpowered, this French Maurice Farman *(below)* typified the planes used earlier in war. When the war began U.S. ranked 14th among the air powers of the world.

The **wild aerobatics** which marked the swirling dogfights of the war imposed severe strain upon the fragile wood and fabric biplanes. Carelessness even in looping, as this old Re-18 *(above)* is doing, could cave in the complicated structure of wood and wires.

American instructor stands before his brightly colored Nieuport fighter in France *(left)*. Planes used by our pilots were mostly castoffs of French air force. Training fields were described as a "horror," and included some of the "worst mudholes in all of France."

21

"Moral and mental disintegration"

in equipment that the majority were rebuilt at the AAF's aircraft center at Romorantin. The heavy and clumsy DH-4 flew with all the grace of an overloaded truck. Pilots were distressed to find a large and fragile fuel tank which could be exploded with a single incendiary bullet, jammed behind their seat. Yet the inferior performance and the pyrotechnic tendencies of the DH-4 did not prevent its use; desperately short of airplanes, we had no choice but to commit these pilot-killers to battle.

Not one of the airplanes the United States delivered to its pilots was really fit to fly in combat. Justice Charles Evans Hughes, upon investigating the American air industry, scored the rampant waste and inefficiency and deplored the "defective organization of the work of aircraft production and the serious lack of competent direction of that work." In the most damning indictment ever received by American industry, Hughes concluded with the regret that *the provisions of the criminal statutes do not reach inefficiency.*

There were only two occasions during World War I when aerial bombing operations did not justly deserve the scorn of ground forces commanders. These were the great air attacks in 1918 at St. Mihiel and the Meuse-Argonne, where General William Mitchell was able to vindicate his theories on the concentration of airpower in a given combat area. On the opening day of the attack Mitchell sent his 1500 planes into battle; he hurled 500 bombers and fighters against each flank of the enemy's St. Mihiel salient, and used the others directly before friendly troops. During three days of continuous air fighting his planes bombed and strafed troops, supply dumps, trains, vehicles and similar targets within 20 miles of the actual fighting.

Mitchell's tactics proved a smashing success, as the startled Germans were harried at every turn by the dense swarm of attacking fighters and bombers. Never once during the reduction of the German salient at St. Mihiel, which was 15 miles deep and 35 miles broad at its base, did Mitchell's air cover allow the Germans to break through and molest the American troops.

Less successful was his operation in the Meuse-Argonne offensive. The night before this attack was launched Mitchell's bombers struck in darkness at enemy airdromes, rail stations and supply depots, and communications centers. As dawn broke his fighters and bombers swept low over the German trenches, hammering at the enemy directly before the advancing American troops. For a limited time Mitchell's tactics demoralized the enemy ground forces; then the Germans responded with hundreds of fighters which wrested air control from the Allied planes. Mitchell noted grimly that the German air force had succeeded in its defense by applying his own theories to the battle front — the concentration of airpower in the combat zone.

Despite the spirited German defense, Mitchell was able to achieve the greatest single aerial triumph of the war during the Meuse-Argonne offensive. On October 9th, Mitchell sent more than 350 bombers and fighters to attack German army reserves which were preparing to counterattack American ground positions. The Allied air armada fought off waves of determined German fighters, and dumped 32 tons of bombs in the heaviest single air attack of the war. Although the total tonnage released was 10 tons less than the maximum load which can be carried by a single bomber today, the sudden attack so stunned the enemy that his planned counteroffensive was never launched.

With full justification an elated Mitchell declared: "...it was indeed the dawn of the day when great air forces will be capable of definitely affecting a ground decision on the field of battle."

The first plane used by U.S. fliers in France; an antiquated Morane Roulier. Ignorance of U.S. officers regarding aviation was at times appalling. One officer, hearing complaints about Caudrons which used wing-warping controls, ordered the planes kept in their hangars, and not allowed to remain in the sun "where their wings could warp."

"Somewhere in France" a mechanic spins the prop of a French-built Spad XIII fighter used by the AEF. Speedy and maneuverable, Spad was selected for production in the U.S. Despite the fact that it was the best Allied fighter of the war (few pilots were lucky enough to fly it), the U.S. declared the plane obsolete, canceled the production plans. Activities of this nature forced the Army to purchase foreign machines. By the war's end, we had bought 4,784 planes of all types from the French government, and American pilots also flew in battle in British and Italian planes. General Pershing condemned failure of United States industry which forced our pilots to fly in "inferior types of planes."

America's ace-of-aces in World War I, Captain Eddie Rickenbacker seated in the cockpit of the Nieuport fighter in which he scored his first 5 victories — and almost lost his life. In the midst of an air battle, Rickenbacker's fighter began shedding its wing fabric, and the wings were on the verge of ripping from the airplane when the pilot barely managed to bring his Nieuport safely to earth. Rickenbacker, who scored 26 aerial victories, was both a brilliant fighter pilot and combat leader. He was the idol of American pilots, and sacrificed opportunities to better his own victory score by boosting his squadron's total. One front-line observer reported that Captain Rickenbacker, as commander of the 94th Squadron, had "perfected the finest flying corps I have ever seen."

Germany's brilliant Red Baron

By late 1915, Germany's pilots had originated pursuit-formation tactics by flying in large gangs which were echeloned for mutual protection. The combination of superior fighters and tactics proved disastrous to the British and the French. Their numerical superiority rendered worthless, the two nations sought frantically to regain a qualitative lead, and throughout the war the fight for technological superiority seesawed back and forth across the lines. But it was always the brilliant Anthony G. Fokker *(left:* his outstanding, highly maneuverable triplane) who set the pace for the rest of Europe to follow. Germany's greatest combat pilot, Baron Manfred von Richthofen *(above)* used his Fokker to good advantage. With 80 air kills, he was the war's greatest ace.

A bad ending to a poor beginning...

The war is over; American DH-4 and Breguet bombers are piled into a giant heap for burning. The destruction of these planes, coming so soon after condemnation of American air industry, caused a major scandal in the United States.

THE GOLDEN AGE OF AVIATION

The appalling carnage of World War I left the American people with a strong aversion to all things military, and in a frantic attempt to return to "normalcy," the nation's huge conscripted Army was disbanded almost overnight. Three years later the Washington naval conference of 1921-1922 sought to reduce navies to impotence. Military leaders felt that the worst blow had come, however, when the economy-minded Coolidge Administration declared itself opposed to military research and development.

Because the paltry defense budget had to stretch a long way, severe competition developed between the Army and the Navy. In their bare struggle for survival the services competed for roles and missions. It is small

wonder that the Navy reacted with such violence to General Mitchell's claims that naval warships could be bombed out of existence. The War Department, top-heavy with infantry, artillery and cavalry thinkers, developed a grim distaste for the small group of veteran airmen who antagonized the General Staff by seeking to advance the airplane as the prime power over the country's traditional military weapons.

No one person so inflamed the War Department and its officers by openly challenging the nation's conservative concept of war as did Brigadier General William Mitchell, who returned from France with a burning ambition and a resolute will to raise the air arm to its "rightful" role in national defense. Mitchell used his position, as well as his talents for writing and for speaking, to spread the gospel of airpower far and wide. He used both bludgeon and rapier to drive home his points; he could be shocking, satirical, irreverent, or all of these together.

Mitchell argued with unflinching logic that the best strategy often dictated destruction and killing at points distant from the ground or naval theater. He acknowledged that the civilians attacked in such operations might include large numbers of women and children, but declared that they were vastly more important as manufacturers of munitions than if they were acting as troops carrying rifles in trenches.

Eventually in the course of World War II the restraining barriers of convention and humanitarian feeling were to collapse completely, and full, although painful, recognition would be made of the reality of "total war."

During the first half of the 'twenties, however, it was Mitchell "against the field." He was a one-man show for air power. He burned brilliantly and defiantly — and then, after he overstepped the bounds of military propriety once too often, his official light was extinguished. But before pressure forced his resignation from the Army in 1926, he planted the seeds of a new doctrine of war and airpower.

Against this background of conflict of doctrine, however, the Army's air officers overcame their enforced poverty of equipment and funds by making daring flights which caught the public's attention and gained for the country immeasurable international prestige. Army fliers consistently set new world records for distance, speed, altitude and load carrying; they flew in the worst weather and over forbidding terrain. Men like Lieutenant J. A. Macready *(left)*, who set a new world's altitude record of 34,508 feet in 1921, were acclaimed by the nation. It was a decade so rich in breaking down the barriers of flight that General Henry H. Arnold was one day to look back in history to declare it "the golden age of aviation."

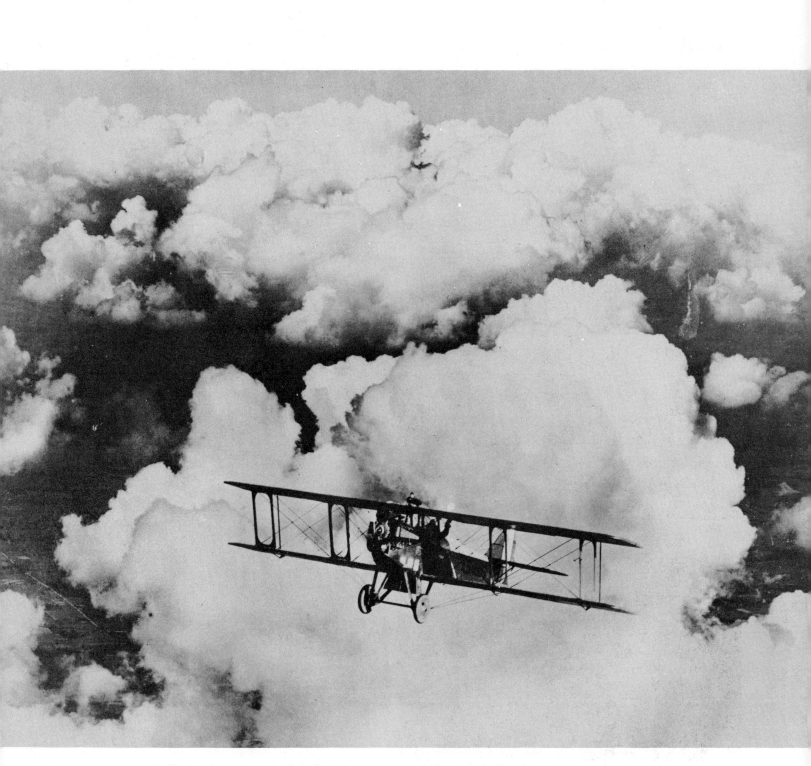

Suffering in an exposed cockpit from extreme cold, receiving barely enough oxygen from a primitive system with a mouth tube, Lt. J. A. Macready *(opposite page)* struggled to world altitude record of 34,508 feet. LePere was one of first "pure research" aircraft.

"The impossible has happened"
Coast-to-coast nonstop in 1923

At 12:36 P.M. on May 2, 1923, the two Army officers pictured above, Lieutenants John A. Macready *(left)* and Oakley G. Kelly, opened wide the throttle of an Army Fokker T-2 transport airplane at Roosevelt Field, Long Island. Grossly overloaded with 780 gallons of gas, the big airplane weighed a dangerous 10,850 pounds. Not a man who watched the single-engined machine lumbering down the runway believed it would ever get off the ground; but at the point where aircraft hangars loomed ahead, the transport plane staggered into the air, virtually scraping its way over the buildings.

The next morning, still loggy from the gasoline remaining in its tanks, the T-2 approached the towering peaks of the Rocky Mountains. Despite their skillful flying, the pilots could not get the pounding Liberty engine to lift the machine high enough to fly above the jagged crags. Undaunted, Macready and Kelly took the clumsy Fokker through boulder-strewn passes and gorges, where a single slip at the controls would have meant a flaming explosion and instant death. Somehow, impossibly, they fought their way through. Several hours later they were over Rockwell Field in California, weary and exhausted, the first two men ever to complete a nonstop flight across the continental United States.

One hundred thousand screaming people greeted the two fliers who had broken all existing world nonstop distance and speed records by flying the 2,520 miles from Atlantic to Pacific in 26 hours and 50 minutes, at the wearying average speed of 94 miles per hour. Among the crowd which offered a thundering ovation at Rockwell Field was the Base Commander, Major Henry H. Arnold, who years later became the Chief of the USAAF. One of the Army's original aviators, Arnold well appreciated the tremendous obstacles which had been overcome and exclaimed jubilantly, *"The impossible has happened!"*

The flight reaped rewards in more ways than one. Macready and Kelly had overcome two heartbreaking failures of the previous year. In proving wrong the experts who had insisted that the flight was impossible, they demonstrated forcibly the growing capabilities of the air service which would one day send its planes to almost every corner of the world.

Missionary zeal and public opinion

One of the major stumbling blocks to the realization of an autonomous and powerful American air force which confronted the Air Service in the decade after World War I was the overwhelming public apathy toward both aviation and the military. The decision to appeal to the public for aid in the struggle to gain military air strength was a necessary one, for all attempts to secure government legislation favorable to the creation of a major air arm had been crushed by the powerful bloc in the Army's General Staff.

The country's fliers were particularly bitter about the Army General Staff, and General B. D. Foulois testified before a Congressional committee that through "lack of vision, lack of practical knowledge, or deliberate intention to subordinate the Air Service needs to the needs of the other combat arms... (the General Staff) has utterly failed to appreciate the full military value of this military weapon."

In 1926, Representative Fiorello H. LaGuardia, carrying on the fight for air autonomy, unleashed the blistering accusation that: "The General Staff are either hopelessly stupid or unpardonably guilty in refusing to recognize the necessity of making a change in aviation."

Whatever the arguments advanced for increased strength, the Air Service had to do with a pittance. It was clear that those who opposed a strong air arm represented the majority in the military establishments and held the positions of military influence. At this stage in the contest for recognition of military aviation, the enthusiasm of the air crusaders could prove no match for the number, the high rank and the power of the opposition.

Defeated on the legislative front, the Air Service determined to demonstrate its capabilities to the man in the street. This could be accomplished only through daring feats which would engage the public's attention. Spurred on by a sense of urgent mission, the military aviators embarked on their program to prove to the American people that aviation was important not only in war, but that it possessed incalculable national value in time of peace.

Thus were created the transcontinental air races, the altitude flights and hazardous long-distance journeys, the good-will missions around the nation and to South America.

The campaign proved remarkably successful; autonomy was still years ahead, but within a decade the United States was well on its way to leading the world in aeronautical progress.

On July 24, 1919, the Army sent this twin-engined Martin bomber on a glorified barnstorming tour of the country. By November 9th the airplane had covered a distance of 9,823 miles along the borders and coastal regions of the United States; actual time in the air was 114 hours and 25 minutes. The historical Round-the-Rim flight gave many thousands a first look at this bombing airplane.

Death was moments away

Of all the new frontiers of flight which challenged the Army's aviators in the years immediately following World War I, none proved so hazardous as the airman's newest realm — high altitude. For Nature designed man's body to remain on the ground, where the atmosphere is rich in oxygen. And of all the things which sustain man during flight, none is more important than oxygen — or its lack.

The airplane pictured above is the experimental LePere designed and built under the direction of the Air Service Engineering Division at old McCook Field in Dayton, Ohio. Powered with the reliable Liberty engine, the LePere was the Army's first aircraft designed expressly for the purpose of penetrating the unknown; in this instance, for flight at extreme altitudes.

The modern flier fears *hypoxia* — a condition in which the body suffers from a lack of oxygen. In the early 'twenties the dangers of hypoxia remained little more than theory, and the only means of learning more of its strange effect upon the human body was to send a man to altitudes where the air thinned out to a dangerous fraction of its sea-level content.

This the sturdy LePere did with gratifying efficiency,

for the Air Service established three world altitude records in its experimental biplane. On October 4, 1919, within a year of the Armistice, Major R. W. Schroeder and Lt. G. E. Elfry established a two-man record by climbing to 31,821 feet. On February 27, 1920, Schroeder flew the LePere alone to set a new record for solo flight of 33,113 feet. And on September 28th of the next year, Lt. J. A. Macready, useing to good advantage a new turbosupercharger geared to the engine, climbed to a new high of 34,508 feet.

Macready suffered considerable pain and discomfort in attaining his new world record. His only source of oxygen was a pressure cylinder attached to a tube with a pipestem mouthpiece which he clenched tightly between his teeth. Flying at a height where hypoxia could render him unconscious within two to three minutes, Macready had to breathe entirely through his mouth. Half of his limited oxygen supply was wasted through exhalation. And it was brutal to have to hold the pipestem clenched in his teeth at *all* times, in an exposed cockpit, with the outside temperature down to minus 60 degrees F.

Evidence of the difficulties faced by Macready in 1921 are found in World War II records. Even with the modern equipment then available, there were 10,000 recorded cases of unconsciousness, and 100 deaths caused by lack of oxygen.

Air mail nobody wanted: our first airway system

The Army's first airmail flight on May 15, 1918, was a preposterous failure, which heaped ridicule upon both the Air Service and the Post Office Department. To begin with someone forgot to fill the airplane's fuel tanks, keeping President Woodrow Wilson (*right,* with Major Rueben Fleet) waiting idly. When the plane finally did take off, it flew in the wrong direction, cracked up 25 miles away on a farm. Two months later the unhappy marriage of the Air Service and the Post Office was dissolved to the gratification of all.

One Air Service project prompted by General William Mitchell was the first mass transcontinental air race (*below*) in which some 60 Army planes participated. The race left wrecked planes strewn across the country in October, 1919, but the winner sputtered home in the record time of 9 days, 4 hours, 25 mins.

Happily, the race proved of long-term value to the nation, for the Army established an intricate network of emergency airfields across the land. The new airway laid the major airfield foundation for future commercial aviation.

Three of the Air Service cross-country race planes at Cheyenne, where mechanics waited to repair and to refuel the ancient machines.

Pipeline in the sky

The innovation in aerial tactics which makes the USAF fleet of some 1,500 medium-range B-47 jet bombers a threat to every city in the USSR is known as air refueling. By transferring fuel from a tanker plane to a B-47, it is possible to remain airborne to a limit decided only by the fatigue of the crew and the successful operation of the engines.

Thirty-four years ago two Army officers, Lieutenants Lowell H. Smith and J. P. Richter, attempted the first air-to-air refueling by hose line from one airplane to another. On August 27, 1923, they took off from Rockwell Field and remained in the air for the astonishing time of 37 hours and 15 minutes, establishing a new world endurance record. To keep their DeHavilland bomber aloft, another plane intermittently flew above and ahead of their own, matching their speed of 90 miles per hour, and passing gasoline into their tank through a 50-ft. hose. The refueling operation was performed 16 times; between 50 and 100 gallons being transferred with each contact.

In remaining airborne for their record-breaking flight of more than 37 hours, Smith and Richter also set a new world distance record of 3, 293.26 miles, a remarkable achievement for their old DH-4B bomber, and an outstanding testimonial to the Liberty engine which powered their airplane. In the ensuing months the two pilots improved their technique and remained aloft for even greater periods of time. Newsreel films of their maneuver astonished theater audiences throughout the country.

But few people realized the extreme danger to which Smith and Richter exposed themselves during each refueling. If even a small quantity of the highly flammable gasoline being transferred from the tanker plane had spilled on the red-hot exhaust manifolds of the lower DH-4B, then both Smith and Richter would have met a fiery death in their fabric-and-dope biplane.

Six years later, using the same technique pioneered in 1923, another Army team astounded the world with a flight lasting more than a week. And in 1949, the B-50 *Lucky Lady II* refueled four times in mid-air to fly nonstop around the world (23,452 miles) in 94 hours and 1 minute.

U.S. ARMY AIRPLANES REFUELING
© H. A. ERICKSON, #425

Speed hops and good-will tours

The dream of pilots — to cross the United States from coast to coast in a dawn-to-dusk flight — became reality on June 23, 1924, when Lt. Russel H. Maughan battled wild headwinds to span the continent in 21 hours, 47 minutes and 45 seconds. Flying a Curtiss PW-8 (above), one of the Army's new "hot" pursuit planes, Maughan landed to refuel five times on his historic flight, found fatigue and nausea from the severe headwinds his greatest problems. He flew the 2,850 miles at an average speed of 156 miles per hour, and established clearly the U. S. fighter's versatility.

On May 2, 1927, three Army amphibians (below) landed at Bolling Field, Washington, to complete a tour of South and Central America which had lasted four and a half months. The good-will air journey proved an outstanding success, and prompted one government official to remark that the flight had done "more good than ten years of diplomatic correspondence."

Five planes left on the flight; two were lost in a midair collision which killed two fliers. It was the only black mark against the tour, which was highlighted by a remarkable 650-mile nonstop trip over the towering Andes. The Loening COA-1 amphibians were seen by millions of South Americans on the air journey which spanned 22,065 miles, and included stops at 25 national capitals.

Army world cruise was elaborate air venture

No one feat in aviation ever prompted greater struggle — or failure — than the first flight around the world. It is a singular tribute to the Air Service, and to the determination of Generals William Mitchell and Mason Patrick, that the Army Air Service in 1924 succeeded in such a venture, where the pilots and aircraft of Great Britain, Italy, Portugal, France and Argentina had failed.

The first globe-girdling flight was rife with more hazards than any pilot wished to admit. It meant the air pioneering of desolate and forbidding parts of the world: arctic ice fields, fogbound ocean areas, steaming jungles, deserts, dangerous mountain ranges; it meant flying through wild storms without radio and with only a minimum of instruments.

Without exhaustive and year-long preparation, the epochal air journey would have been doomed to failure from the start. But the Air Service gained the co-operation of 22 foreign governments, and secured for the global planes 40 landing fields around the world, each stocked with provisions for emergencies. The Douglas company built an excellent machine (right) for the attempt.

The four Douglas World Cruisers took off from a lake near Seattle (below) on April 6, 1924. For the next 175 days they fought their way around the earth, covering a total distance of 27,553 miles in 15 days, 11 hours, and 7 minutes actual flying time, cruising between 53 and 103 mph. The return of two planes on September 28th to Seattle marked the close of a brilliant chapter in Army flying history.

Icebergs off the bow

One of the miracles of the round-the-world flight was that all the men who left returned alive to the United States, despite the loss of two of the four planes which originally attempted the journey. The four men who successfully maintained the tour were feted wherever they landed, like Lt. L. H. Smith *(right)* in Japan.

One plane smashed into an Alaskan mountainside; the crew walked away from the wreck, spent ten agonizing days suffering from intense cold and snow blindness before they reached natives. The final leg of their return was made in an Eskimo bidarka *(lower left)*.

The two planes which completed the trip narrowly missed destruction over the Atlantic; in a thick fog, they barely scraped over an iceberg.

World speed records and a burst of glory

Few other events could better emphasize to the public the capabilities and the performance of military airplanes as did the annual air shows and air races which began in the United States in 1920. That was the year that France took permanent possession of the trophy for the International Gordon Bennett Race, leaving racing pilots without a competitive event in which to perform.

In 1920, the Pulitzer Brothers, in order to promote the development of United States aviation, established the Pulitzer Trophy Race, which became air racing's bonanza competition for the next six years.

Private contestants for this prize (as well as others to be won in the air meets) quickly were eliminated by soaring costs of aircraft, fuel, parts and salaries; the fight became a pitched battle between the Army and the Navy. For five years victories seesawed between the two services; then the Army Air Service announced that 1925 was to be its last year of competitive air racing. When that year's event was over, enthusiastic Army pilots held in their grasp not only the

In somewhat untraditional flying gear for Army pilots, a victorious Lt. Russell H. Maughan stands before the racing plane in which he won the Pulitzer Trophy on October 14, 1922. (Maughan later made the famous Dawn-to-Dusk transcontinental flight.) Taking off in a Curtiss racer *(below)* is Lt. Lester J. Maitland, who placed second in the 1922 Pulitzer race, behind Maughan. Maitland also became world famous for his aerial exploits in the Army; with another pilot, he made the first U.S. to Hawaii flight.

coveted Pulitzer trophy, but several new world speed records as well.

For the 1925 Pulitzer race the Army and Navy flew the same airplanes; specially built Curtiss R3C2 racers; victory thus would fall to the pilot with superior air skill. The Army's Lt. Cy Bettis copped honors by beating out the Navy's Lt. Al Williams with an average speed of 248.9 mph. Actually, the new record improved only slightly the previous year's mark; strong winds and new rules against power dives to gain speed, curtailed Bettis's performance.

Several weeks later Lt. James H. Doolittle replaced the wheels of Bettis's plane with pontoons, and thundered over a closed speed course to win the Schneider Trophy with a record-breaking 232.6 mph. The event was doubly significant, for Doolittle, in the Army's first entry into the Schneider race, whipped British, Italian and two U. S. Navy hopefuls. The Army had never before entered any seaplane race.

Still hungry for more records, Doolittle then flashed his little fighter down a straightaway course to crack the world seaplane record with a new average speed of 245.7 mph.

These annual air races and the other yearly special air events and shows became picture windows for the American public to view their air service in action, and to see the skill of its pilots. Massed bomber formations demonstrated battle tactics; fighters flew mock air battles; parachutists thrilled the crowds with skillful descents; and the precision aerobatics of pilots in teams of stunting fighters kept hundreds of thousands of people gasping in awe.

A Curtiss P-1 fighter plane whips around the pylon on the John L. Mitchell Trophy Race *(right)*, which featured a course demanding of the highest piloting skill. Massed crowds at air races saw Army pilots fly fighter planes as well as special racers. At *left* is Lieutenant Ennis C. Whitehead, who became famous in W. W. II for his leadership in the Southwest Pacific as an AAF general officer. Many pilots who flew in races later became AAF leaders.

Aerial daredevils

If the record-breaking flights of the early 'twenties convinced the public that a great new age in the air was dawning upon the world, then the daredevil stuntmen of flying were equally effective in proving that the air belonged to men of great courage, steel nerves and, many believed, empty heads.

Immediately after the war hundreds of fliers with little money and great enthusiasm snatched up war surplus airplanes at bargain prices. These were the gypsy fliers who created the famous barnstorming era when planes toured the country, landing on farms, fair grounds and country roads to bring aviation to the grass roots of America.

The thrills farmers received from watching flimsy airplanes whirling about in aerobatics soon wore thin; to keep their fuel tanks and stomachs full, pilots went to desperate lengths to satisfy the rural public's craving for something unusual. And the public got more than it ever bargained for.

As a plane circled low over a field packed with spectators, one man climbed out of the cockpit and went through a variety of breath-taking stunts guaranteed to make even the stoutest heart falter. Men stood on their heads on wings, passed from one plane to another, dangled on rope ladders, hung by one hand from a wing tip or the undercarriage. But far and away the most startling maneuver was the "breakaway," in which a man appeared to fall off the wing tip of a plane to certain death below. While women fainted and men cried out, the man who had fallen to a terrible end grinned and hauled himself back into the airplane via a cable and harness which were invisible from the ground.

Most famous of all aerial stuntmen was Omar Locklear (above), former Army lieutenant and flying instructor. Locklear was absolutely fearless in the air, but he had only a few seconds to decide whether or not it was all worth while when, in 1920, he plunged to his death while stunting before movie cameras.

Less thrilling, but unquestionably safer, were the parachute jumps made by many Army and civilian fliers. Army men clinging to DH-4 wings (left) tumbled off into space to awe crowds before opening their chutes and drifting to safety.

Few thrills were greater than the sight of a man tumbling through space *(above)* to what seemed to be certain death, as this Army flier is doing. Yet the early parachute jumps made by Army personnel were to prove invaluable for the development of safer equipment and improved jumping techniques, which eventually saved the lives of many fliers in distress. For sheer entertainment and the hope of seeing a man plunge to the earth, the crowds flocked to see stuntmen like Lt. Omar Locklear. At *right*, Locklear hangs from wing of a Jenny, and *(below)* he transfers in mid-air to another plane.

While Army trained for war, it aided science and country

The development of the Army's air strength extended beyond its war maneuvers and testing of new equipment. Every effort was made to utilize military aircraft for the public, and Army planes flew special mercy missions in the years between the wars. On September 16, 1920, four bombers carried relief supplies to persons isolated by floods at Corpus Christi; in February, 1923, an Army pursuit plane flew a doctor over frozen Lake Michigan to aid a dying man; and on March 4, 1924, four Army bombers blew open with bombs an ice jam in the Platte River at North Bend, Nebraska.

The period following the war saw a progressive evolution in the tactics of pursuit aviation. This was the most vital area of airpower, claimed General Mitchell, because the primary aim of pursuit was to destroy the enemy's air force — thereby permitting all other branches of aviation to perform their special duties. Nothing could resist pursuit aviation, Mitchell explained, because it was designed to attack other planes from every possible angle; no large, lumbering aircraft could provide adequate defense against fighters. Toward this end, the Air Service practiced constantly. Mock air combat duels, like this attack of a Thomas-Morse fighter against a Martin medium bomber, gained proficiency for the Army's pilots.

The value of the airplane as an aid to science was well estab-. lished in the early 'twenties. Of especial merit was its ability to carry scientific instruments to great heights for the study of atmospheric and other phenomena. The solar eclipse *(above)* was photographed at 9:11 A.M. on January 24, 1925, by Dr. S. M. Burka *(below)*, flown by Lt. G. W. Goddard of the 8th Photo Section.

Strategic bombing in the early twenties was an obscure theory which forecast future giant air fleets smashing enemy homelands. Unfortunately for heavy-bombardment aviation during this period, the prophets ignored performance characteristics of existing or projected aircraft. The models of this era were almost universally underpowered, bomb loads were small in relation to plane size, and planes were short-ranged. Despite these shortcomings, the Army was paving the way for the future bomber by special tests, like the dropping of 4,000-lb. bombs from this Handley-Page bomber *(above)* at the Aberdeen Proving Grounds in September, 1921.

One of the greatest peacetime Army contributions to the country was the aerial Forestry Patrol which began in June, 1919, and, because of lack of funds, ended in 1926. In the first four years when Army pilots flew patrols over the Oregon and California forests *(above),* they discovered 2,000 forest fires, saved untold millions of dollars' worth of standing timber. Oregon alone reported a 62% drop in major fires after Army started its operations.

The period 1918-1927 doomed once and for all the captive balloon for aerial observation, artillery spotting and other activities in direct support of infantry and other Army operations. The disappearance of the dangerous and unpredictable balloons was hailed with relief, especially by men who had to run for their lives when the unwieldy objects burst into flames. The rare photo *(below)* at Fort Sill, explains why haste was so often necessary.

Mitchell vs. the Navy

Until the advent of the military airplane, the lines of demarcation and responsibility between the Army and the Navy regarding coastal defense of the United States were relatively simple and clear. The rise of aviation vastly complicated this defense situation, and touched off a fierce battle between the two services regarding authority and service capabilities which to this day has never been entirely settled.

In the 1920s both services were already operating their own air arms, each of which had been developed independent of the other. The ranking officers of both the Army and Navy held fast to their concept that airplanes could never play anything but a subordinate role in war; to the Army the infantry was the Queen of Battle, and to the Navy the battleship reigned supreme.

When, however, there arose the question of what the new medium of war — airpower — could do to the

In a scene which could be right out of W. W. II, the battleship USS *Alabama* (above) rolls hard over from a direct hit with an 1100-lb. bomb. At *top right*, a Martin MB-2 bomber hits the crow's nest of the once-mighty battleship with a phosphorus bomb before other planes sink her with 2,000-lb. bombs. *Right center:* A 600-lb. bomb scores a direct hit on battleship USS *New Jersey* during the 1923 tests off Cape Hatteras, North Carolina. *Right:* Few other pictures have portrayed the enormous power of the bombs used by Mitchell's planes so graphically as this shot of the battered and helpless USS *Virginia;* the battleship is gutted inside and is a total wreck.

Navy at sea, the Army brass judiciously took a back seat and allowed their flying subordinates to set their sights against Naval power and authority. To the General Staff it was a splendid opportunity for the Army to gain even more power that it possessed; the air enthusiasts who scored the helplessness of the Navy to protect the continental United States against attacking enemy airpower could only enhance the prestige of massed ground forces and artillery.

General William Mitchell was more enthusiastic about the capabilities of aviation against ships than

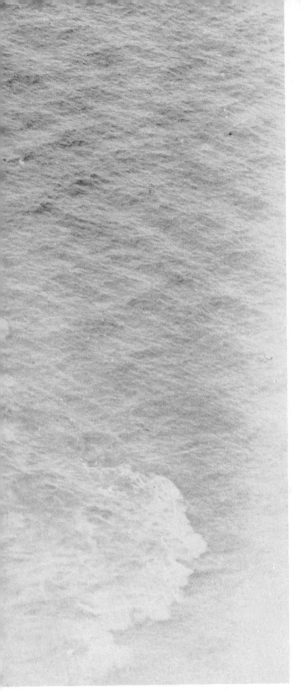

**Brigadier General
William Mitchell**

frustration, he successfully arranged for actual bomb-dropping tests against retired naval ships. Small vessels were easily destroyed in these experiments, but the successes were decried by naval authorities who stressed the light armor and structural fragility of the lesser warships.

Mitchell was undaunted, and his triumphs came in

against any other kind of target. He had "destroyed" the Navy many times over in his writings and speeches, and seapower was ever a fair target for his barbed eloquence. To him and his followers in the Air Service, Mitchell worked out a simple formula for the aerial defense of the United States coastlines. It involved, first, reconnaissance by air to locate approaching air forces and surface fleets; second, a series of sky battles to determine control of the air; third, after control was attained, direct attack on enemy vessels. He worked out a plan of co-ordinated action for the third phase, which was to remain the ideal plan for concerted attack on ships for many years. It involved simultaneous action by low-level attack planes (using cannon and machine guns against deck personnel), high-level bombers (dropping special-purpose armor-piercing projectiles or depth bombs), submarines (guided to torpedo attacks by director aircraft), and torpedo bombers.

The basic plan seemed simple enough, but the key question remained: How effective would such an attack be against well-manned, armored vessels? Mitchell pointed to certain theoretical considerations which favored the airplane, such as the power of the initiative derived from its superior speed. He drew attention to the terrific explosive power of an aerial bomb as compared with a cannon shell of equal weight, and asserted that the accuracy of high-level bombing exceeded that of coast artillery at twelve-mile range. Finally, after considerable haggling, name-calling, and weary months of

The bombing tests of 1921 and 1923 served to do more than merely to sink the target ships. For the first time air planners came to appreciate the devastating effects of certain kinds of missiles against naval targets, and examinations of ships like this study of damage aboard USS *Alabama* paved the way for improved bombs.

The mighty German battleship Ostfriesland, called unsinkable by naval authorities, takes a bomb off her bow during 1921 tests.

the subsequent devastating strikes which smashed, and sank, the most powerful warships ever built in the world up to that time.

The major tests of 1921, for which his men trained for three months, shook naval complacency to its foundations. On June 21st the attacks began against captured prizes from the German imperial fleet, 100 miles off the Virginia capes. The submarine U-117 went down in 16 minutes. On July 18th, Martin MB-2 bombers dropped fourteen bombs to sink the German light cruiser *Frankfurt* in 30 minutes. But the most decisive phase of the 1921 tests occurred on July 21st when seven of Mitchell's bombers, each carrying a 2,000-lb bomb, smashed the huge German battleship *Ostfriesland* (called unsinkable by seapower strategists), making the ship roll over, and sink in a bare 21½ minutes.

The defensive cries of the Navy and its supporters served only to confuse further the entire picture of airpower *vs* seapower. In 1923, Mitchell's planes returned to erase any doubt as to their capabilities against even the largest warships. On September 5th, off Cape Hatteras, the powerful USS *Virginia* and the USS *New Jersey* were sent to the bottom with shocking ease. Two other battleships also received mortal blows which dispatched them beneath the waves.

Of course, as the Navy explained feverishly, those vessels had been towed out into open water, were incapable of maneuver, and were unarmed and unmanned. But even the admirals were abashed at the destructive power shown by aerial bombs against the stoutest naval armor. General Mitchell, in any event, was thoroughly convinced. After the tests he declared without reservation that existing types of airplanes could, with negligible loss to themselves, seek out and destroy all existing classes of seacraft. He was largely supported in this sweeping claim by the official conclusion of the Joint Army and Navy Board, which had been approved on August 18, 1921. The Board confirmed, among other things, that existing aerial bombs could sink or seriously damage any existing type of vessel. Adequate quantities of bombers were seen by the Board as possibly the *decisive factor in coast defense*. In any future attack upon the American coast, the Board concluded, the Navy must share with the air arm its primary function as the first line of defense.

The Navy reluctantly agreed (it had little choice) that coastal defense should be shared with the Army and Air Service. But in what manner? What constituted the surest and most efficient arrangement for co-operation?

General Mitchell set forth an entire new concept of coastal defense which virtually swept the Navy bare of its cherished authority in this area. The Air Service's General Mason Patrick agreed heartily with Mitchell, and declared as early as 1921 that the Army air arm could take over coastal defense, that it could perform all the functions of shoreline patrol, sea search and attack on hostile vessels.

Each military service claimed the right and the ability to discharge the responsibility for the coastal defense of the United States; and, if the bombing tests against ships conducted by Mitchell proved the power of his airplanes, they also launched several decades of confusion of responsibility, unwholesome service rivalry with bitter name-calling and accusations, and a duplication of facilities and functions which could hardly be avoided under such conditions.

In the years subsequent to the battleship trials, the War and Navy Departments continued their battle in the no man's land of overlapping jurisdiction. Time after time efforts were made during the interval between wars to delineate precisely the respective responsibilities of both for coastal defense, but all failed to dispel the ambiguity and conflicting interpretations that persisted right up to Pearl Harbor — with all its disastrous consequences.

The unsinkable battleship Ostfriesland on her way down. Less than 22 minutes after the first of seven 2,000-lb. bombs smashed in her hull and pounded huge holes in her deck, the heavily armored German vessel rolled over and sank. Destruction of the German dreadnought was most decisive of Mitchell's air attacks.

AIRPOWER COMES OF AGE—TESTS REPLACE THEORY

Despite demobilization up to 95 per cent in early postwar years, small appropriations and an emphasis on pursuit aviation, the development of medium bombers progressed significantly over World War I models. By the late 1920s Keystone bombers, shown *(above)* in massed formation with the 2nd Bomb Group, and Curtiss Condors, had become the new Air Corps' standard bombardment aircraft. Increased performance of the new mediums permitted development of mass-bombing techniques, as the 2nd Bomb Group demonstrates, and the wide use of bombers around the world. A Keystone B-3A *(right)* passes over Coron Bay, Philippines.

Field trials scored obsolete equipment

A major cause for the virtual abandonment of the attempt to develop strategic airpower in the immediate postwar period was the failure of heavy bombers to measure up to the sanguine expectations of airpower enthusiasts. The bomber planes flown in June, 1926, showed little improvement over the Martin MB-2 of 1920; planes remained underpowered, carried small bomb loads, and had limited ceilings. They could fly barely 300 miles from their bases to strike at an enemy; this was sufficient only for medium-bomber tasks.

The outstanding bomber of the 1919-26 period was the Curtiss Condor *(left;* with attacking fighters) built in 1924, but still a first-line aircraft in 1930. A biplane powered by two

600-hp engines, and with a top speed of 132 mph, it was hardly the weapon to fulfill strategic prophecies.

Despite this lack of proper equipment, the Air Corps worked hard to develop the most realistic tactics for employing its obsolescent air fleet. The Air Corps' mission was accepted as providing maximum support for ground forces, and in this respect pilots became proficient in tactics which promised effective results against enemy ground troops and equipment; an example in striking power is seen in the photo *(opposite page, bottom)* of 30-lb. white phosphorus bombs exploding on a California target range.

The airpower theory of the late 'twenties assumed the necessity for day raids and assumed that control of the air, made possible by pursuit superiority, would allow bombers to fly safely in daylight and to bomb accurately with small losses.

Formation flying in the standard inverted V was prescribed for mutual defense against enemy pursuit planes; note the formation *(bottom)* held by three Curtiss B-2 Condors as they pass over Inspiration Point in Yosemite National Park in California on a simulated bombing mission. Flights of this nature gave pilots valuable experience over the wildest terrain, and gained the Air Corps the ability to fight anywhere in the world.

Automatic flight controls were presaged by this Air Corps test of April 24, 1930, when a Curtis B-2 Condor bomber was flown entirely by robot control. Note pilot standing in cockpit, hands clasped.

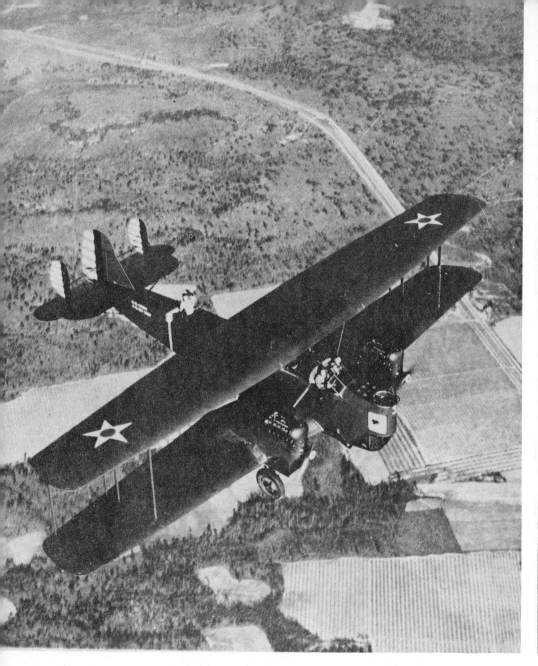

The art of bridge-busting—three decades ago

Virtually every bombing technique employed by the USAAF during World War II owes its existence to the training and the maneuvers conducted by the AAF's predecessor organizations — the Air Service and the Air Corps. One technique in particular which enjoyed overwhelming success during the war was that of bridge-busting, the not-so-gentle art of smashing the concrete, steel and wooden spans upon which an enemy depends for rapid communications over culverts, gorges and rivers. Entire armies in the European, Mediterranean, Pacific and Asian theaters of combat were decimated by Allied firepower once our tactical planes had accomplished the vital task of isolating the battlefield from reinforcement and supply.

On these two pages are three of the world's rarest airpower photographs — the bridge-busting experiments conducted by the Air Corps in December, 1927, a series of tests which proved invaluable through the knowledge imparted of the effects of high-explosive bombs against large steel and concrete spans.

The bombing tests were held with Keystone LB-5

twin-engined bombers — one of the Air Force's two major bombardment weapons in 1927 — stationed at Pope Field, near Fort Bragg, North Carolina. The target was the Pee Dee River Bridge, which the Army Engineers had been ordered to destroy. The opportunity to smash at so lucrative a target in an age of critical financial want by the Air Corps was snatched at eagerly.

The Keystones made attacks singly, in formation, at varying altitudes and with different bomb sizes — all carefully planned to yield the greatest possible data on the most successful methods of reducing the powerful bridge structure.

In the *top left* picture, one of the Keystone LB-5 bombers which participated in the attack is seen returning to Pope Field. The photograph at *lower left* reveals the excellent accuracy achieved during the bombing runs. A three-plane formation salvoed their 600-lb bombs from an altitude of 6,000 feet just before this picture was taken; note the explosions directly against and near the bridge. In top photo, a 600-lb. bomb has just struck as a near miss.

Special bombing tests proved the value of attack aviation

Three years after the interdiction strike tests against the North Carolina Pee Dee River Bridge, the Air Corps conducted a series of experiments to improve its offensive capabilities against an enemy air force. In November, 1930, Davis Ridge of Camp Stanley in Texas was lined with obsolete Army aircraft, all placed in the same line-up positions they would occupy if the airfield were operational. From a safe distance Air Corps and Ordnance observers watched the first large-scale airfield bombing experiment in this country.

The experiment was an unquestioned success. During the morning of November 3rd, attack and light bombers roared low over Davis Ridge in the Camp Stanley area, flying simulated minimum-altitude missions. As the first wave raced by, a series of explosions rocked the area *(opposite page, bottom picture)*, and mushrooming

An obsolete fighter plane explodes in a shower of flames from the direct hit of a small demolition bomb during the low-altitude-attack tests held on Davis Ridge, Camp Stanley, Texas on November 3, 1930. The planes on the ground were attacked under simulated combat conditions, with a time limit imposed on the striking force. Before the attack was over, every plane had been destroyed.

flame enveloped several of the targets. One after the other, sometimes singly and now and then in formation waves, the light and attack bombers made their "surprise attacks." Plane after plane was blown into wreckage, until finally there remained only the charred skeletons of the "enemy" fighters and bombers.

Airfield attacks had been carried out in the World War, but rarely were they executed with the intention of gaining air superiority by destroying the enemy air force on the ground. The Camp Stanley experiments determined also the bomb sizes most effective for setting aflame or destroying by blast enemy planes caught in exposed positions. Bomb weights ranged from 17 lbs. upward. Fragmentation, general demolition, and other types of missiles were also employed, and their effectiveness noted for future reference.

The lessons learned from the 1930 simulated combat strikes had a profound influence on attack aviation in the Air Corps, and to this day the swift, light bomber, flying at treetop height to hit the enemy, with the tactical advantages of speed and surprise, remains one of the most important aircraft types in the USAF.

One of the most valuable lessons gained from the 1930, and subsequent, tests was that the greatest destruction could be achieved among parked aircraft by using a special type of bomb — the fragmentation missile which descends slowly by parachute and explodes at ground height. In this manner the greatest possible blast effect is realized, and the target aircraft receive a severe mauling through the pieces of red-hot steel which flail the area.

Long before the advent of Pearl Harbor, the Air Corps had developed its low-altitude tactics to a fine art. The effectiveness of this technique was never better demonstrated than in the war to come — as we shall soon see.

An old DH-4 bomber disappears beneath a black smoke cloud *(top)* as a direct hit destroys the airplane. Note the charred wreckage of planes which have been totally gutted by flames. Aircraft types destroyed in the bombing maneuvers included both light bombers and fighter airplanes. A 17-lb. bomb explodes a plane in flames *(right)* during the early phase of the ground-attack test.

"The most beautiful fighter airplane ever built," is the accolade earned by Curtiss's sleek and graceful P-6E fighter. A favorite of pilots everywhere, it was one of world's best fighting airplanes. Nine P-6Es of the 17th Pursuit Squadron from Selfridge Field hold a perfect line-abreast formation above clouds.

With most of their number obscured in thick dust clouds, Curtiss P-1 fighter planes of the First Pursuit Group thunder down a dirt airstrip in a mass formation take-off. Hardy and maneuverable, the P-1 was the "granddaddy" of the famous *Hawk* series which continued to World War II fighters.

With the new airplanes of the late 'twenties and the early 'thirties came fighter aircraft of sleek lines and powerful engines — the biplane Boeing and Curtiss fighters which pilots remember with nostalgia. Three Boeing P-12E fighters of the Air Corps' *Skylarks* aerobatic team "cut loose" high over the earth.

On the morning of June 28, 1927, an Army Fokker tri-motored transport plane with the improbable name of *Bird of Paradise* lifted sluggishly from a California airfield and headed for Hawaii, 2,418 miles away. Twenty-five hours and 50 minutes later Lt. Lester J. Maitland and Lt. Albert F. Hegenberger stepped onto Wheeler Field, Honolulu, the first men ever to fly nonstop from the U.S. to the Hawaiian Islands.

Following successful aerial refueling flights which set world endurance records, the Army studied the air-to-air technique for its possible military use. On September 1, 1929, tests were held with the Boeing *Shuttle* and a Douglas tanker, shown over Cleveland. The Boeing pilot was Captain Ira C. Eaker, who seven months before had been co-pilot of the record-breaking *Question Mark*. Refueling plane also served *Question Mark*.

Careful and extensive preparation went into the flight of the *Question Mark* which, in January, 1929, broke all world endurance records by remaining aloft for one week. In this picture, taken on December 17, 1929, over Bolling Field, Washington, D. C., the Fokker transport is refueled in air tests by the Douglas tanker plane. Improving on the mid-air-refueling techniques developed in 1923, Army's pilots eventually developed the art into an indispensable weapons system.

Army's planes consistently broke world records, opened new airways

With each passing year, the Army's planes and pilots continued to break world speed, altitude, endurance and other flight records. In-flight refueling ultimately developed beyond the stage of an interesting experiment to assume valuable merit as a new means of extending greatly the range of bombers. Although the men who pioneered the technique could hardly have dreamed of its wide future application, it was the true beginning of a weapons-system concept — the basis of the modern USAF. This doctrine views the military airplane as only one part of a major team, all elements of which are necessary to deliver destructive agents to the enemy. In respect to air refueling, this would involve the weapons carrier, the tanker, the air and ground crews, and the equipment and logistics required to keep the entire team functioning.

In the late 'twenties Army pilots also chalked up new distance records for fighter planes. Lieutenants R. W. Douglas and J. E. Parker each flew a Boeing PW-9 fighter *(above)* from France Field, Canal Zone, to Washington, D. C. Another Boeing fighter, a P-12D, made scientific history in 1931 *(below)* by remaining aloft for hours at extreme altitude with cosmic-ray equipment.

"Question Mark" brought U.S. Army highest praise

No other single event in aviation so startled the world in 1929 as the news that an Army transport plane had taken off on January 1st, and remained aloft for nearly one full week.

Behind the banner headlines proclaiming the astonishing feat were long weeks of preparation and strict training in mid-air refueling techniques. The airplane was the same type Fokker C2-3 transport which, in 1923, had flown nonstop from the United States to Hawaii. On January 1, 1929, it took off from Los Angeles to remain airborne for the incredible time of 150 hours 50 minutes and 40 seconds. The grueling training proved its worth, for the tanker airplane, flown for the most part by Captain Ross G. Hoyt and Lieutenant Odas Moon, transferred 80,000 lbs of materials to the Fokker in 43 aerial contacts.

Included in the 40 tons were 5,660 gallons of gasoline, 245 gallons of oil, batteries, other supplies, and meals for the five men aboard the *Question Mark*.

Only after its port motor cut out because of plugged grease outlets, did the Fokker return to earth from its 11,000-mile journey.

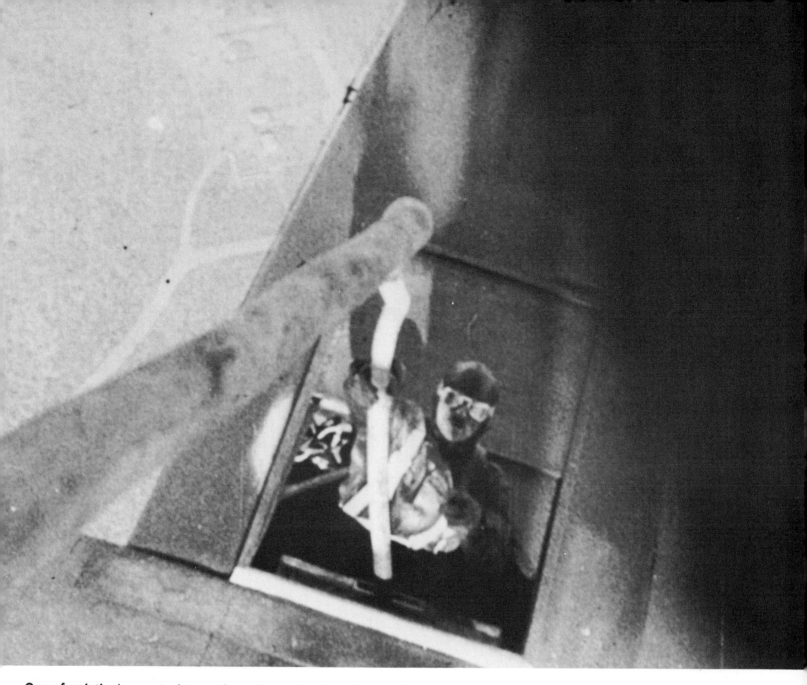

One of aviation's rarest pictures shows Captain Ira C. Eaker reaching up to grasp the fueling hose as it descends from the Douglas tanker; 5,660 gallons were transferred during the week.

Left to right: Capt. R. G. Hoyt; Capt. I. C. Eaker; Maj. J. E. Fechet; Maj. C. Spaatz; Lt. E. R. Quesada; M/Sgt. R. W. Hooe. Hoyt flew the tanker, Fechet was then the Air Corps chief.

Precision formation flying in line-abreast formation is demonstrated by pilots of the 27th Pursuit Squadron, Selfridge Field, Michigan, flying speedy Boeing P-12E fighter planes. One of the most famous fighter lines in aviation history, the P-12E served the Air Corps well for many years. Just prior to W.W. II, the then-old and weary planes were used for radio-controlled targets.

New observation planes of the early 'thirties featured clean design, high performance. One of the Air Corps' best was O-25C.

Air corps extended its fighting ability to include all terrain, all kinds of weather. Ski-equipped P-1C takes off on winter maneuvers.

Parachute jumping advanced from a perilous adventure to the stage of a fine art, and men like Corporal Garland Cain became experts at tumbling from airplanes through space. Corporal Cain demonstrates the proper positions for leaving the wing of an airplane. He grasps wing strut, leans back. He then releases one hand, extends his body away from plane. In final sequence, he has cleared wing and is ready to open chute.

Beyond the wild blue yonder

The tremendous object soaring high over South Dakota is the stratospheric balloon *Explorer I,* which on July 28, 1934, carried three Air Corps officers to 60,613 feet. Sponsored jointly by the Army Air Corps and the National Geographic Society, the *Explorer I's* sealed gondola carried Major W. E. Kepner and Captains A. W. Stevens and O. A. Anderson to a strange new world where the air seemed to disappear and the hostility of open space beckoned.

When the Army and death flew the mails

Under Presidential order the Army Air Corps flew the United States mail for the brief period extending from February 19 to June 1, 1934. It was one of the saddest episodes in the history of the American air force, for fourteen pilots were killed during that unhappy and ill-fated attempt to maintain commercial mail schedules over unfamiliar territory and with a motley collection of ragged transports, fighters, and bombers, such as the Curtiss Falcon *(above)*.

The winter of 1934 was about the worst in history, pilots recall. Along the Great Lakes region, blizzards screamed down from the north with blinding snow and intense cold. Pilots encountered more of the same over the jagged Rockies, and the Northwest became an aerial no man's land of violent flying weather.

Within the first three weeks of flying the airmail in tactical planes with their primitive equipment and open cockpits, nine pilots and passengers went to their death. Such a violent outcry was raised that for the next nine days all planes were ordered off the mail runs. When they returned to flying status, it was with little improvement.

Single-seat fighters with scanty instruments were used to fly at night and in weather which would have grounded the most modern air transports. Pilots scanned ice-rimmed instruments with flashlights, froze in exposed cockpits, and too often found their frail ships unable to overcome the violent storms. Old B-6 bombers struggled against headwinds at ground speeds of 60 mph. And pity the men who flew ancient Curtiss Condors and Ford trimotors dangerous to pilot even in calm weather!

Among the Army pilots who flew the air mail in 1934 was Robert L. Scott *(left)*, then a lieutenant in the Air Corps. Scott, who in later years became one of the Air Force's outstanding combat pilots, and who today is a brigadier general, often flew the dreaded "Hell Stretch" — from Chicago, to Cleveland, to Newark. During the few months of airmail flying, Scott had two roommates killed and, finally, moved in with another man who had lost three of his closest friends on the airmail runs; they figured nothing could happen to either of them after that. Scott missed death by the barest margins. Several times he was forced down. Two nights when other men were killed and he was overdue, Scott was given up for dead.

"The grand Old Man of the AAF," is the way millions of airmen have described General Henry "Hap" Arnold. His career so closely parallels the development of the United States Air Force that the story of the man is at once the unceasing struggle for American airpower. In 1911 Arnold as a lieutenant attached to the Signal Corps became one of the Army's first flying instructors. With the handful of farsighted pioneers then piloting the Army's ancient machines, he contributed to the development of new equipment, planes and techniques which spurred the growth of the air organization and kept it alive during its darker moments. His name is identified with many of the Air Force's outstanding accomplishments — including the famous Alaskan Flight of B-10 bombers to that area in 1934, which he commanded *(above)*. In 1942 he became Commanding General, AAF, and later rose to five-star rank.

AIRPOWER YOU CAN TOUCH

In the year 1926, instructors at the Army Air Corps Tactical School preached heresy to their attending students. The primary mission of military aviation, they stressed, was not the defeat of hostile aircraft in the air or the acquiring of intelligence information for the use of ground forces. Instead, the faculty proposed that the intrinsic purpose of airpower was to eliminate the enemy's ability to wage war by neutralizing his air force and by destroying his vital centers.

The proposals were startling contradictions to the accepted role of airpower held by the Army General Staff and the War Department. The threat of official disapproval and of disciplinary action forced many airmen in key positions into covert methods of spreading their air philosophy. These were hardly effective means of dissemination, and more than seventeen years were to be required for the theory to achieve validity — which came, not in the classroom, but in the air battles high over Europe.

The "new warfare" presented as doctrine in the early 'thirties actually was not original; indeed, it had long been preached by Mitchell and others. But technological break-throughs in the development and the production of new weapons afforded tremendous advances in performance; for the first time the airmen's visions seemed assured of fulfillment. As a consequence, even though the War Department still refused to recognize airpower as more than an auxiliary force, the Army's air leaders plunged ahead eagerly in their gospel, confident that future events would prove them accurate prophets.

The year 1930 saw the initiation of new bomber-design advances which mark this date as the major turning point in bomber development between the two world wars. The success of Boeing's B-9 and Martin's B-10 medium bombers, incorporating clean all-metal, monoplane, retractable landing-gear designs, with resulting high performance, gave the Air Corps the two finest bombers in the world at that time. It was their success which broke down the barriers impeding the eventual realization of strategic airpower; both these planes opened the way to still faster and larger designs, aircraft with the range and the bomb load to make strategic airpower more than the wistful dream it had been for so many years. The two new planes demonstrated further that size could be increased without loss of aerodynamic efficiency — and in one fell swoop engineers found their open-sesame for the development of bigger and faster bombers. Heartened by this success, the Air Corps in 1933 issued a design proposal for an even more advanced multi-engined bomber.

The only manufacturer willing to gamble with a new concept was Boeing, which submitted a radical four-engine bomber design. The Boeing airplane incorporated all the best aerodynamic features which had been developed during the previous decade — and it was successful beyond anticipation; the sensational B-17 Flying Fortress, the airplane which during its combat history not only devastated the industrial heart of Germany, but destroyed the remaining barriers which stood in the way of the development of the true strategic air force we now possess.

Here, at last, was the kind of airplane fondly dreamed of by the air planners . . . a long-range, self-defending offensive terror of the skies — truly, a Flying Fortress. General Henry H. Arnold later wrote that the B-17s were not just prophecies or promising techniques; they were "for the first time in history airpower that you could put your hand on."

The rising pressure for air-power equality forced the Army on March 1, 1935, to establish the General Headquarters (GHQ) Air Force, a major step forward in the development of modern air strength. This administrative success was no panacea for the ills which stunted the growth of the American air arm, but the GHQ organization — which provided a mobile combat air force co-ordinate with the four ground armies — was the first real progress toward the autonomous air arm of today.

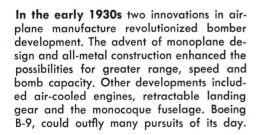

In the early 1930s two innovations in airplane manufacture revolutionized bomber development. The advent of monoplane design and all-metal construction enhanced the possibilities for greater range, speed and bomb capacity. Other developments included air-cooled engines, retractable landing gear and the monocoque fuselage. Boeing B-9, could outfly many pursuits of its day.

Martin B-10 outflew world's best fighters

The Air Corps Act of 1926 signalized the beginning of an intimate association between the Air Corps and the aircraft industry, by providing for design competitions among manufacturers preliminary to drafting developmental contracts. By 1930 the Air Corps was able to take advantage of its marriage with industry, and issued a design proposal for an advanced heavy bomber. The results greatly heartened the proponents of bombardment aviation, for six leading manufacturers submitted design bids which showed startling aerodynamic improvements.

Clearly the most exciting entry was the Martin B-10, a mid-wing, all-metal monoplane with retractable landing gear and a power nose turret, which gained excellent performance through structural refinements and reductions in air drag. It was a plane that looked, as well as acted, the part of a modern bomber. When tested in 1932, the Martin showed a speed of 207 mph and a ceiling of 21,000 feet. Its over-all performance rated it as the fastest and most powerful bomber in the world. Field tests with the B-10 in ensuing years, such as winter oper-

ations in February, 1936, at New Hampshire (below) proved conclusively that the United States had forged ahead in bombardment weapons — a lead that was never to be relinquished.

Both the Martin B-10 and Boeing's B-9, established new world standards of performance and design, and sent the Air Corps well on its way toward future air strength which, in time of need, could cope with anything threatened by foreign powers.

Unfortunately, however, in 1931 these technological advances marked the only front on which victory had been gained. In 1931 there were only 1,500 planes in the Air Corps, and barely 39 of these could truthfully be regarded as bombing airplanes of any merit. The struggle to gain strength in numbers was one which continued right up to the opening days of World War II. When Franklin Roosevelt became President of the United States in 1933, the Navy acquired a staunch champion, and for years neither Roosevelt nor his cabinet paid much attention to the Army, much less its airpower needs. Following a conference with the President in 1935, General Billy Mitchell, who had noticed that Roosevelt's desk was covered with naval mementos, said unhappily: "I wish I could have seen one airplane in that collection."

An unprecedented long-range mission and a severe test for the Air Corps' new B-10 bomber was made in the summer of 1934, when Lt. Colonel Henry H. Arnold led ten of the Martin bombers on a grueling 7,360-mile round-trip flight from Washington, D. C., to Alaska and return. The airplanes left Washington on July 19th *(above)* with orders to photograph strategic landing sites, to determine the usefulness of a major air force in Alaska in time of emergency, and to prepare an over-all report on northern frontier defenses. En route to Alaska the bombers made refueling and supply stops at Patterson Field, then at Minneapolis, Winnipeg, Regina, Edmonton, Prince George and Whitehead, arriving July 24th at Fairbanks. From this base the planes photographed 20,000 square miles — a strip 400 miles long and 50 miles wide — mapping airways in and out of Russia, and from across the Arctic Circle. The only accident occurred on August 3rd when a bomber sank during a forced landing in Cook Inlet *(below)*; the crew escaped without injury and a week later the plane was flying again. The other B-10s flew home nonstop from Juneau to Seattle.

New attack aviation forecast its WWII role

By 1933 the Air Corps had acquired a modern attack bomber, the Curtiss A-12 which could carry six machine guns and 400 lbs. of bombs. Fragmentation bombs *(above)* spill from bomb racks.

One of the major innovations developed by the Air Corps for its attack aviation was the parafrag bomb, which enabled airplane to escape effects of blast. A-12 *(right)* releases eight of new missiles.

A-12 Shrikes line up for 1936 winter maneuvers at New Hampshire. Dissatisfied with A-12's speed and bomb-carrying ability, Air Corps pressed for new designs with greater speed, bomb load.

U. S. attack bombers were outclassed

Designed as a direct replacement for the A-12, Northrop's sleek A-17A attack bomber gave the Air Corps the performance it lacked in older ground-support models. In 1936 the airplane served with distinction, but so rapidly did aircraft performance improve that by 1939, when it was still the Army's major attack bomber, the A-17A had been hopelessly outclassed by new German machines. This was no reflection upon the ability of the American air industry, or Northrop in particular (Japanese engineers who studied purchased Northrop bombers declared them the world's finest aeronautical engineering products); the deficiency in airplane performance was rather a consequence of niggardly appropriations, and an inexcusable apathy on the part of the President and the Congress to heed the threats of a powerful German air arm. In 1939, the United States was no better than a third- or fourth-rate air power. Roosevelt's first Secretary of War, George H. Dern, was openly hostile to airpower and denounced the concept of destroying armies or populations by air bombardment as "the phantasy of a dreamer." It was this myopic perspective which committed American pilots to war in 1941 in inferior airplanes.

In prewar days the Air Corps trained constantly in chemical warfare. An A-17A on field maneuvers in October, 1941, swoops low (above) over troops caught by surprise with simulated gas attack. Inspection of A-17A bombers (left) of 17th Attack Group in 1941.

An achievement which stood for two decades

Standing as one of the great scientific flights of all time, the ascent of the Air Corps' *Explorer II* stratosphere balloon on November 11, 1935, brought Captains Albert W. Stevens and Orvil A. Anderson to the unprecedented height of 72,395 feet. No other balloon ascent until 1956 ever matched this incredible feat, and no men have ever remained so high for an equal period of time; the rocket planes which today soar into the stratosphere do not linger. Sealed in a 9-ft. pressurized gondola at a height where their blood would have "boiled" had pressurization failed, the two officers contributed heavily to scientific knowledge of cosmic rays, the solar spectrum, upper atmospheric phenomena and the earth's curvature. They took 15,000 photographs and won the National Geographic Society's coveted Hubbard Medal.

The Explorer II towers high *(right)* over the base camp in Strato-Bowl near Rapid City, South Dakota, prior to launching. *(Bottom)* Gondola of balloon has just touched earth. Ripping open the balloon prevented wind from dragging sphere along ground.

The Explorer II over South Dakota. Altitude record of 72,395 feet is second highest.

Captains Orvil A. Anderson *(left)* and Albert W. Stevens pose before *Explorer II* gondola.

The first all-metal pursuit to go into production for Air Corps, Boeing's stubby P-26 fighter set military speed and altitude records from 1932 to 1934. Shown is a combat formation maneuver by 20th Pursuit Group.

With a top speed of 234 mph, the chunky P-26 was Army's first-line fighter plane around the world until delivery of newer P-35 and P-36 fighters. Army purchased 139 of the Boeing fighters; eleven others were used by the Chinese against Japanese fighters. In December, 1941, Philippine Air Force flew hand-me-down P-26s; pilots fought courageous but futile battles against Japanese.

The standard Air Corps bomber in 1938-1939 was the Douglas B-18 Digby, shown flying over the snow-capped peak of Mount Ranier, Washington *(usually reserved for Boeing)*. With a maximum speed of 215 miles per hour, the B-18 was a sturdy and dependable airplane, albeit somewhat slow and lacking in the performance which characterized the crop of new bombers that appeared just before the war. A development of the DC-2 commercial transport, the B-18 was replaced for combat by newer airplanes.

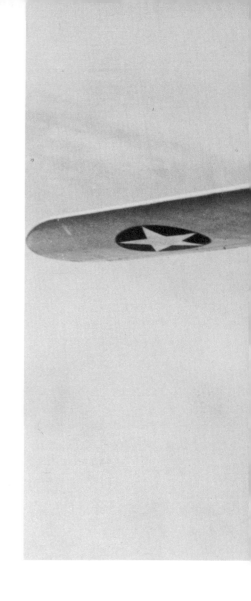

Fall of France spurs air training program: 33,000 pilots in 1941

Many of the Army's pilots of the late 'thirties gained their flying proficiency in trainers like this North American BT-9 (*left*), banking steeply behind the camera plane. Pilot training program increased from 500 per year in 1938 to 33,000 pilots for 1941.

High above famed Randolph Field, a student pilot holds his PT-19 in inverted position (*above*) as he follows through a series of aerobatic maneuvers. Students graduated from primary trainers like this PT-19 to basic trainers, then went on to advanced flying.

Best known of all primary trainers was the Stearman/Boeing *Kaydet* biplane series. The first move into the air for green students, the brightly painted planes were given wide and respectful berths by all other pilots, in anticipation that—"anything might happen."

A new generation of American fighters

By the end of 1936 the Air Corps had emerged from the poor state of pursuit aviation to which it had been reduced by being forced to fly obsolete, slow and inferior fighter airplanes. The new Seversky P-35 and Curtiss P-36 fighters which pilots received were well-designed, modern airplanes, able to fulfill their tasks admirably. Unhappily, this advantage proved only temporary, for by 1939 these new fighters had reached the peak of their development. The newer Bell P-39s and Curtiss P-40s which the Air Corps received in 1940 and 1941 were designed to fulfill the mission of defending this country's shores by attacking enemy landing boats and troops. As such they were excellent airplanes, and well suited for this role. They had excellent speed at low altitudes, carried tremendous firepower, and could absorb heavy punishment from enemy fire. Unfortunately, during the war these characteristics were not wholly adequate against the high-performance enemy fighters which were designed specifically to fight at great altitudes. The P-39 and P-40 lacked superchargers, not because of technical difficulties but because the Army thought them "unnecessary." It was this failing in planning — and not design inadequacy — which later brought so much abuse upon these two fine machines.

P-36A attack formation. One of best fighters in its day, it was obsolete by WWII.

The Curtiss P-37 was an Air Corps experiment to gain the speed advantages of clean aerodynamic lines of the liquid-cooled engine, mated to a P-36 fuselage. This rare photo shows the P-37 during cold-weather tests at minus 12° F. at Ladd Field, Alaska.

Clean design of Airacobra shows clearly *(above)* in photograph of early model. Lockheed's twin-boomed P-38D Lightning *(below)* which entered production just before war, was first of the "great American fighters." Lightning featured speed above 400 mph, outstanding rate of climb, ceiling above 40,000 feet, heavy firepower. It was AAF's first fighter able to best German and Japanese fighters under almost any conditions.

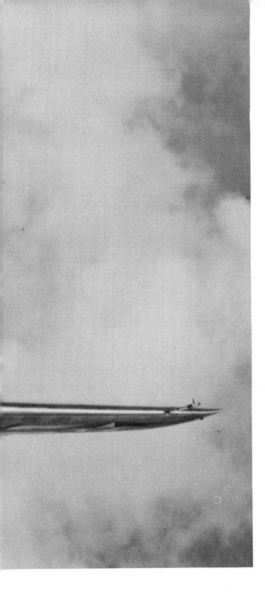

Curtiss P-40 Tomahawk could absorb brutal punishment; was excellent fighter-bomber.

Airacobras on 1941 maneuvers in the Carolinas *(above)*. Russians called P-39s the best low-altitude attack fighter of the war. Seversky P-35s *(below)* were first of modern Air Corps fighters, by 1941 were outclassed by German Messerschmitt, Japanese Zero.

Flying Fortress revolutionized airpower

If one single airplane can be said to symbolize airpower, the Flying Fortress is the most logical choice. First flown in 1935, Boeing's new B-17 design proved more than just another airplane; it was an aerodynamic revolution wrapped up in a slim fuselage and four engines. It carried bombs internally, could span long distances at extreme height, featured defensive machine guns fired from enclosures in the fuselage. It could lose two engines and still fly and fight, and it achieved unprecedented accuracy through its Norden or Sperry bombsights. Most important, however, was the seemingly limitless potential for improvement of the basic aircraft.

The one great fault of the B-17 before the war was its scarcity. Despite AAF pleas for more planes, production was held to a minimum. By Pearl Harbor, AAF had only 114.

To demonstrate to the public the new miracle of the B-17, pilots of the 2nd Bomb Group in 1938 and 1939 toured the nation. The first 12 B-17s flew 9,293 hrs. and 1,000,-000 miles without a single serious accident.

There was a long and successful road ahead for the B-17 from early models like the one flown in 1937 (*above*) at Wright Field in Ohio. Twenty-two years after its first flight, the B-17 is still serving with the USAF.

Air Corps new Mitchells, Marauders and Havocs proved worth as powerful medium and light bombers

In one prewar field especially the Air Corps enjoyed considerable strength — the quality of its medium and light bombers. Three airplanes — the Douglas A-20 Havoc, North American B-25 Mitchell, and Martin B-26 Marauder — were available in some quantity before Pearl Harbor, and served successfully in almost every combat theater of the war.

The Havoc was a 1937 design built to meet French air needs, and in 1939 it had no peer in the world. Not even the vaunted light bombers of Germany's Luftwaffe could match the Havoc's speed, firepower, bomb load and, especially, its rugged construction.

North American's B-25 Mitchell was always a favorite with pilots — as it is even today. An "honest" airplane at the controls, it combined outstanding flying characteristics with, in later models, the greatest forward firepower of any airplane flying — fourteen heavy machine guns, bombs and rockets. Its ability to meet any local climactic or geographical conditions made it a natural to fight for the AAF around the world.

Martin's B-26 Marauder enjoyed no such popularity in the earlier days of its life. A "hot" airplane that would kill an unwary or incompetent pilot, it was promptly dubbed the *Widow Maker* and *The Incredible Prostitute*. The latter title arose from the fact that because of the smallness of its wings in proportion to the plane's size, it seemed to have "no visible means of support." Notwithstanding its serious teething troubles, the Marauder went on to turn in brilliant service during the war.

The Japanese produced medium bombers which were faster and which could fly farther than this AAF trio, and Germany's spectacular Ju-88 managed to perform admirably in many roles other than that of a bomber. But the combat records of the three American planes clearly marked them as the best of their kind in all World War II.

Marauder was to serve as primary medium bomber *(above)* in ETO, as well as fighting in Africa, Pacific, Alaska. Havocs *(left)* fought with British, French before AAF service as light bomber.

Shown on prewar maneuvers, Mitchell was most popular medium bomber in AAF. An excellent desert bomber, it also served with distinction in Pacific jungles, in China, and in the Far North. Most famous raid made by airplane was strike against Japan.

Hickam Field: 7 December 1941

WAR FINDS AAF UNF

The first eight months: defeat and disaster

On the morning of December 7, 1941, some crude leaflets fluttered down on the flaming carnage of Oahu. They said, *"Goddam Americans all go to hell."*

This abysmal effort at psychological warfare proved one thing — that in 1941 the Japanese knew as little about us as we knew about them.

Here is where mutual ignorance ended, and the hard facts of life became unavoidable. The Japanese raid against American installations in the Hawaiian Islands was a military masterpiece. Military orders of the day called for us to be on the alert; and no evasive eloquence can alter the fact that the Japanese caught us off guard.

Millions of words of testimony have attempted to place the blame on those responsible for the Pearl Harbor debacle. Unfortunately, political considerations have transcended the straightforward recital of military events, and the countless accusations and countercharges have only further confused the matter.

The simple truth is that: "December 7th . . . will live as the date of one of the most brilliant military performances of all time." The Japanese achieved complete surprise. While morally reprehensible, they struck "swiftly, boldly, and accurately..." with 353 carrier-based airplanes, and sank or rendered useless the battleship fleet upon which the Navy relied to protect our Pacific shores. Japanese pilots either destroyed or crippled more than 150 Navy airplanes; they shot eleven Navy bombers out of the sky without loss — eleven fully armed planes that never fired a shot in their own defense.

Japanese planes destroyed 141 Army fighters and bombers, and damaged many more. They set aflame and demolished hangars, storage shops and warehouses, barracks, piers, cranes, munitions dumps and other vital installations. The final result of the attack was that the Japanese, for the trifling loss of only 29 airplanes and 55 men, destroyed more than 300 American aircraft, wiped out our airpower in the Hawaiian area, rendered impotent all but the carriers and submarines of the Pacific battle fleet, shattered island installations, and killed or wounded more than 4,000 Americans.

The most significant point of the Pearl Harbor attack is not the local victory that the Japanese achieved, but rather the brilliant fashion in which they applied their airpower. Never before in history had there been such precise and effective use of tactical air weapons. Of the 353 planes launched by the six aircraft carriers of the Nagumo Force against Pearl Harbor, only 154 went after our ships. The remaining 199 fighters and bombers strafed and bombed airfields, to the end that the attacking Japanese force might enjoy local air superiority.

It is astonishing, then, that the Japanese failed to exploit their tactical victory. By not following up the success of their air attack with an invasion to occupy our Hawaiian bastion, they forfeited anything more than a temporary gain.

REPARED

Pearl Harbor attack: "superbly planned...superbly executed"

On the first day of World War II, the United States lost two thirds of its aircraft in the Pacific, yielding air superiority to the enemy. Hawaii was effectively eliminated as a source of immediate reinforcement for the Philippines. And on those beleaguered islands, enemy attacks rapidly whittled down our remaining air strength until it could do no more than annoy the victorious enemy.

Japan controlled as much of the vast China mainland as she desired at the time. She soon captured Guam and Wake. She dispossessed us in the Netherlands East Indies, enveloped the British in their Singapore bastion, and almost entirely eliminated that country as a military threat. Within a few months fearful anxiety gripped Australia, and its northern towns shook beneath Japanese bombs. Enemy planes swarmed almost uncontested against northern New Guinea, New Ireland, the Admiralties, New Britain and the Solomons. Enemy occupation of Kavieng, Rabaul and Bougainville not only threatened the precarious supply lines from the United States, but became potential springboards for the invasion of Australia itself.

At no time during those first dark months were we able to more than momentarily check the Japanese sweep. The bright sparks of heroism in a sea of defeat were not enough, and too often we were willing to see victories

accomplished where nothing of the sort had occurred. Our national pride stung to the quick, we grasped at straws to prove that what was happening was impossible — that this defeat could not be ours. In those terrible early days, we were guilty of finding heroes and victories where neither existed — we sank imaginary warships and shot down nonexistent planes.

Throughout the war the Allied peoples scorned German claims that they had sunk the British aircraft carrier *Ark Royal* — three times — while the vessel still floated and fought. In our own wartime communiqués American forces four times "sank" the Japanese battleship *Haruna*.

There is no question about it — in the first year of war it was the United States which committed its pilots to battle in machines outclassed by those of the enemy. The reluctance of our government in prewar days to heed the lessons of extraordinary advances in German and Japanese air power cost us dearly in lives — and men died for no reason other than their country had blundered by underestimating a potential enemy.

Yet, despite their initial overwhelming military successes, the Japanese never enjoyed a real opportunity for ultimate victory. Within one year of the opening day of war we had grasped the initiative. The overwhelming numerical superiority which the Japanese enjoyed (largely by destruction of our own forces with relative impunity) began to disappear. By the spring of 1943 we had regained the advantage of quantity and — of far greater importance — we enjoyed a definite qualitative superiority in weapons.

The gutted wreckage of a P-40 fighter at Wheeler Field. Here 151 warplanes, including 75 new P-40 fighters, stood wing to wing, inviting attack. Fearing possible sabotage, authorities had removed fuel and ammunition from the newly-delivered fighter airplanes!

America's proudest bomber, a new B-17, lies broken in two with the pieces flung about, outside of Hangar No. 5 on Hickam Field.

Eventually the United States triumphed — and the Japanese suffered total disaster. The reasons for this were many. The Japanese superior airpower was a bright but short-lived flame. Their airplanes quickly were outclassed by new American products. At their best they could employ but a mere fraction of our engineering skill which, when released from the shackles of low priorities and niggardly appropriations, soon changed the course of history. And they lacked anything similar to the American air industry which expanded with explosive speed.

But at the heart of all the reasons why the Japanese — and the Germans — failed, was that neither country understood the strategic potentialities of airpower. Therein lies their defeat. They thought of airpower in terms of an attack weapon to be used only as support for naval forces and ground armies; Pearl Harbor was a brilliant tactical victory, but a strategic failure. It destroyed American battleships which posed no threat to Japanese industry — but it left unscathed our industrial potential to wage war. Pearl Harbor was a battle won — and a war lost.

Because neither the Japanese nor the Germans had a valid formula for the use of strategic airpower, they overlooked the possibility that it would be used against them — and so they were unprepared to counter the great fleets of B-17s and B-24s over Germany, and the fire-sowing B-29s over Japan.

In the early days of the war there were enormous gaps in American airpower — gaps which were filled at a high price. The eventual victory gained was a tremendous tribute to American airpower, but especially to those men in the prewar Air Corps who had planned so far ahead.

For every single fighting plane the Army Air Forces used in World War II either was flying, or was under design, *before* the first bomb fell against Pearl Harbor.

One of the B-17s which arrived in the Hawaiian Islands during the Japanese attack, its pilot managed a forced landing at Bellows Field.

Curtiss P-40 lands at Kunming, China *(above)*. P-40s bore brunt of early fighting, used skillful tactics to beat nimble Zeros. Bell

P-39s refuel *(below)* in Australia after Jap raid. Designed for ground support, Airacobra was outmaneuvered by agile Zero.

First of the "great" American fighters, Lockheed P-38 Lightnings *(above)* entered combat late in 1942. Japanese said it was most feared and hated of all AAF fighters. These P-38Fs are flown by sergeant-pilots, the "White-Haired Boys of General Arnold." Republic P-43 Lancer *(below, with AAF crew)* was used by Chinese. Serious mechanical difficulties of airplanes disgusted Chinese fliers.

"... their flight was one of the most courageous deeds in all military history."

VICE ADMIRAL WILLIAM F. HALSEY

A boost for our morale

Few events in American military history have so stirred Americans as the daring air attack of sixteen B-25 medium bombers against the Japanese homeland on April 18, 1942. The heart of Japan was struck during one of the darkest periods in our history, when Japanese forces stormed triumphantly across a vast island and ocean front of twelve thousand miles, when Americans died — many in inferior airplanes — and a country we had always regarded as second-rate was teaching us some fine points in how to fight a war.

The attack against the major cities of Japan in 1942 was the result of co-ordination between the AAF and the United States Navy, which carried the medium bombers aboard the carrier USS *Hornet* to within launching distance of the Japanese islands. It was a move on the part of the U. S. Navy which was fraught with tremendous risk, for the attack admittedly was carried out solely for the purpose of bolstering a sagging national morale, and

the Navy could ill afford to lose the USS *Hornet* and her accompaning carrier, the USS *Enterprise*. The credit for this successful venture is shared by all, from James H. Doolittle, who led the air mission and earned the Congressional Medal of Honor, to the hapless Navy crewman who had an arm sliced off by a whirling B-25 propeller aboard USS *Hornet*.

But there is an untold side to this story. Japanese intelligence had anticipated a carrier attack against Japan, and several hundred fighter planes waited in ambush for Doolittle's bombers. Only an incredible error in radio transmission on the part of a Japanese bomber pilot — who had sighted Doolittle's planes in the air, winging toward Japan — averted disastrous failure. The raid was over and the B-25s racing for China before more than a handful of fighters were able to take off.

Halsey's carriers turned and fled the moment the B-25s were airborne. It was well they did — for bombers and fighters of the 26th Air Flotilla from Kisarazu Air Base already were moving out to attack, and the same Nagumo Force which had shattered Pearl Harbor was racing to intercept our carriers.

On the day of take-off, Doolittle's bombers faced heavy swells which crashed high over *Hornet's* bow, drenched planes with spray. A Navy gun crew watches anxiously as *Hornet,* her bow rising rapidly under pounding seas, virtually flings one of the B-25s into the air. All sixteen airplanes made take-off without any accidents, although several of the bombers dropped dangerously near the water immediately after clearing the deck.

First plane off — Doolittle's B-25 — climbs rapidly away from *Hornet (left)*. Bombers flew to Japan at 15-20 feet height, hit home islands with complete surprise; Japanese called these tactics "brilliant." Bombers struck Tokyo, Kanagawa, Yokohama, Yokosuka, Kobe, Osaka and Nagoya. To evade attacking fighters, one B-25, flew beneath electric power lines to shake off pursuers.

With spray crashing over the deck, a B-25 prepares for take-off. Plans for raid were so secret that bomber crews were unaware of their final destination until aboard *Hornet*, on way to Japan.

The Japanese held a special hatred for the men who flew B-25s in the Southwest Pacific. Seemingly without nerves, B-25 pilots thundered in at treetop level to hit Japanese targets in the New Guinea-Lae-New Ireland area during early 1942. They were one of the few bright lights in an otherwise dark picture. Here two Mitchells race away from their bomb run against a Japanese field.

The fight against heavy odds

The beginning of the long road back in the Southwest Pacific meant fighting against enemy planes which in many respects could outfly our own. The medium bomber and fighter pilots who hit the Japanese in the New Guinea area fought a savage jungle air war against heavy odds; rarely did our planes return unscathed from their missions. It was an air war which, unhappily, made aces out of the Japanese fighter pilots based at Lae and Rabaul.

The best way to destroy Japanese fighters was on the ground — like this Zero (above) in flames on a New Guinea airfield. Patrolling P-39 Airacobras (left), although outmaneuvered and outclimbed by Zeros, had superior diving ability and heavier fire power. Unlike Zero, P-39 could absorb heavy damage, keep fighting.

U. S. Navy evens the score

The Japanese attack in June, 1942, against Midway Island called for the destruction in battle of the American Pacific Fleet, and the invasion of Midway to extend to the east Japanese warship and bomber patrol lines. Simultaneously, occupation of Attu and Kiska islands in the Aleutians would block United States raids against the Japanese mainland. That the Japanese grand strategy was turned into an overwhelming defeat which cost the enemy more dearly than our own losses at Pearl Harbor had hurt us, was due to brilliant U. S. Navy air action.

Army B-17s (*above*, taking off from Midway) helped locate the Japanese fleet, but failed to hit any enemy ships with bombs. The Navy, after suffering terrible air losses in the early fighting, found its opening and struck swiftly. In a single day dive bombers sank four great enemy carriers, downed hundreds of planes, and killed hundreds of irreplaceable first-line airmen. It was the pivotal airsea battle of the war; it broke the Japanese Navy's back, and avenged Pearl Harbor.

Japanese carrier, Kaga, swerves *(above)* beneath B-17 at 20,000 feet; photo taken by 431st Bomb Sq. Skillful maneuvering *(below)* by *Kaga's* captain avoids several salvos of heavy bombs dropped by Fortresses from 20,000 feet. No AAF bomber struck enemy.

Long-ranging B-17s were credited by Japanese as one of major factors in Allies' staving off defeat in 1942 *(above)*. Ability of B-17 to defend itself and to fly long distances to search out enemy movements, admitted the Japanese, deprived them of element of sur-

prise in battle. The war wasn't all fighting, as these P-39 pilots *(below)* in Carribean area discovered. They sat out months of waiting for an attack against Panama Canal which never materialized. Bombers operating from Canal Zone were used against German subs.

Forgotten air war in the north

Few parts of the earth offered so bleak and desolate a fighting front as the cold and fog-shrouded islands of the Aleutians chain which stretches westward from Alaska. In June, 1942, under cover of planes from the aircraft carriers *Junyo* and *Ryujo,* the Japanese occupied Attu and Kiska islands. Bombers and fighters raided Dutch Harbor in Alaska, but with little effect. Soon the Japanese and the Americans discovered that the screaming winds, snow, fog and cold of the Aleutians were deadlier foes than each other. The enemy occupation of Attu and Kiska went unopposed, for there existed grave weaknesses in the American defense force. The extensive uninhabitable areas made it virtually impossible to establish an aircraft warning service; the emergency build-up of radar installations early in 1942 was far from finished when the Japanese attacked. Inaccessibility of sites by road, the necessity of moving equipment by small boats through ice packs, the difficulties of working under conditions of almost constantly bad weather — all these combined to hamper defense activity. Once the Japanese were entrenched on Attu and Kiska, however, they had good cause to regret their move. The same conditions which assailed our own forces tied down Japanese aircraft, troops and ships. With each passing month our airpower build-up meant only inevitable defeat for the enemy. Initial light raids by fighters and bombers gave the dug-in Japanese a preview of the future; as air-base facilities expanded, four-engined bombers moved in. Enemy installations were hammered heavily *(above;* bombs explode on piers). However, our pilots considered it a "stinking way to fight a war," and they feared the Japanese less than their own operational problems, like the pilot of this flaming P-38 *(below)* which crashed in high winds on Adak Island.

AAF TAKES OFFENSIVE

August 1942: First ETO heavy bomber mission
November 1942: AAF covers African invasion
August 1943: AAF, Navy air at Guadalcanal

The destruction of much of the German war machine by heavy air bombardment was a task accomplished at heavy cost in manpower and materiel. It was an incredibly successful campaign of thirty months by the AAF which allowed the recapture of occupied nations and the final devastation of Germany itself at a cost of life which, though heartbreaking, was relatively low compared to the appalling casualties suffered in World War I trench warfare.

During the afternoon of August 17, 1942, twelve Flying Fortresses of the 97th Group, 8th Bomber Command, attacked the Sotteville rail marshalling yard at Rouen, France, to launch the AAF heavy bomber offensive against Germany. With at least half of the bombs falling from 23,000 feet into the target area, the raid "far exceeded in accuracy any previous high-altitude bombing in the European theater by German or Allied aircraft." It was an auspicious beginning. Flak was light, German fighters proved no trouble for the heavily armed B-17s, and the only casualties were two crewmen who were slightly cut when a pigeon smashed into their airplane's nose on the return flight to England.

The precision bombing of heavily defended Nazi Europe was the most critical job of World War II, and it was not accomplished without serious errors in judgment, which sometimes cost us dearly in planes and men. The German air force defended its nation with grim determination, and our losses rose steadily as the enemy threw more and more of his air strength and anti-aircraft into bomber defense. Indeed, by the beginning of 1944 the Germans were employing fully two thirds of their entire fighter strength in home defense — leaving but a third of their fighter strength for all other purposes, including support of their armies on the gigantic Eastern Front.

For a while this defense attained such effectiveness that the Germans restricted us to shallow penetrations of their homeland. One year after the first raid against Rouen, we lost 59 bombers over Schweinfurt and Regensburg — more planes than we lost in the first six months of bombing. In October, 1943, over Schweinfurt, out of 228 attacking airplanes, we suffered 62 heavy bombers shot down, 138 heavily damaged, 539 men killed or captured, 40 wounded, and some two dozen planes so badly damaged they never flew again.

For three months our bombing campaign was severely inhibited. Then, in a remarkable technological achievement, the P-51 fighter was modified to attain the range necessary to escort our bombers anywhere in Europe; with the P-38s and P-47s also flying escort, we beat the Germans down, and by 1944 we roamed the air over the entire continent.

The two years — from August, 1942, to September, 1944 — were a time of trial and error. We had much to learn. But we did the job, and at the end of the war the German military economy was shattered, and the country prostrate.

Silhouetted against the contrails streaming from hundreds of other bombers, two Fortresses ride in ghostly formation for Brussels factories, heavy machine guns ready for action against enemy.

Bomb bays open, B-17G *(left)* of the 452nd Bomb Group on its target run is bracketed by heavy flak over Ludwigshafen. Flak bothered B-17 crews less than German fighters; Me-410 *(below)* is less than 25 feet off Fortress's wing during attack against Brüx oil plants. More than 100 fighters swarmed over bombers as they hit fuel plants.

A task to be done

By 1943 the AAF had focused and clearly defined the purpose of its ETO bombardment campaign. First came the defeat of the Luftwaffe and the destruction of German fighter defense. Second was destruction of the primary targets: the aircraft and ball-bearing industries; chemicals and oil; synthetic rubber; sub yards and bases; motor-vehicle plants. The need was plain, but it was not always possible to concentrate on the proper targets. There was much abuse of airpower; bombers supported troops, hit V-weapons sites, bombed sub pens — giving the resourceful German time in which to repair damage and re-establish his flow of materiel. This was one of the costliest mistakes of the entire air war; we did not learn until late in 1944 that a target had to be hit repeatedly to keep it from being rebuilt.

This decision to send bombers against targets other than primary industrial objectives — aiding local battle situations or the sea war, but avoiding factory damage, and permitting industry to continue its flow of war goods to the front — may have prolonged the war by months. An example of this faulty planning: of the 2,638,000 tons of bombs dropped on all German targets by the AAF and the RAF, only 48,000 tons — or 2 percent — were directed against aircraft plants.

Riding high above a towering smoke column from the flaming Astra Romana Oil Refinery at Ploesti, Rumania, a Convair B-24 Liberator of 15th Air Force begins long return flight to home base. Dr. Albert Speer, German Reichminister of Armament, admitted that "planned assaults on the chemical industry which began on May 12, 1944 . . . was the most decisive factor in hastening the end of the war. The attacks . . . would have sufficed, without the impact of purely military events, to render Germany defenseless."

Flying Fortress looms over the Focke-Wulf FW-190 fighter aircraft Components Plant and the two Karl Borgward Motor Transport factories at Bremen (left). The attack against the German air force was carried out by our fighters and bombers both on the industrial front and in air-to-air battle. By late 1944, German aircraft production was concentrating almost entirely on defensive fighter planes. Every effort was exerted by German industry to increase fighter production, thereby robbing troops of bomber support, and other essential industry of vitally needed materials. Dr. Albert Speer admitted after the war that he could have increased fighter production by another 50% except for devastating effects of precision bombing.

Almost complete destruction of the Focke-Wulf Assembly Plant *(below)* and storage area at Marienburg, Germany, was achieved in heavy bomber attack by 8th Air Force on October 8, 1943. Almost all the assembly sheds and machine shops have been destroyed by blast and incendiary effects. Dense shower of heavy bombs also destroyed dozens of airplanes waiting for assembly in, and around, the industrial structures. In February, 1944, 8th Air Force conducted unprecedented five days of intense bombing against the German aircraft industry. Attacks seriously disrupted the production of almost all aircraft plants.

Bombs away! A salvo of 500 pounders *(above)* from Liberators of 463rd Bomb Group, 15th Air Force, heads directly for the rail marshalling yards at Bekes-Csaba, Hungary in September, 1944. Constant blows at German rail system snarled communications.

On August 1, 1943, 177 B-24D bombers of Ninth Air Force flew from North Africa bases to strike at vital Ploesti oil fields in Rumania. Planes flew at minimum height *(below)*, were given savage beating by AA fire, dozens of intercepting enemy fighters.

The intensity of the German antiaircraft fire thrown up at our bombers was beyond all description — and this one picture of a B-24 Liberator which has just emerged from a flak barrage over Vienna best portrays the plight of bombers which "didn't make it." Note the left inboard engine; trailing white smoke at this moment, it soon burst into flames, tearing off the wing and sending the B-24 down in a fiery streamer. Courage of German fighter pilots often astonished bomber crewmen — Messerschmitts and Focke-Wulfs plunged heedlessly through their own flak to hammer at our planes. The fighters drew the highest toll of our bombers.

Liberator formation is dwarfed by black smoke rising from Xexia oil refinery at Ploesti (*above*) during attack of August, 1944. In cramped working space, B-24 navigator (*below*) checks position over Germany as his bomber begins long flight home to base.

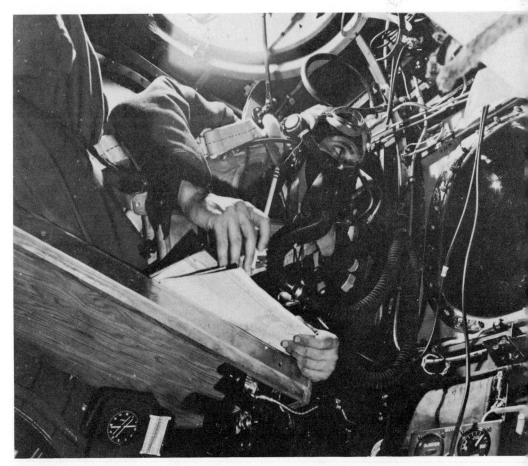

Weary crew of Flying Fortress deplanes after long mission deep into Germany *(above)*. Return of bombers meant all-night work for ground crewmen like Sgt. Arthur Dyer *(below)*, B-24 mechanic.

The all-night workers

When the bombers returned from their long missions over German targets, work was just beginning for thousands of mechanics, armorers, radiomen, and the other maintenance personnel without whose skill there could be no campaign to destroy Germany from the air. There were, actually, two crews for the big planes — the men who flew, and those who tended the complex machines. Maintaining the B-17s and B-24s in the best possible condition was an enormous task which required tens of thousands of skilled men who cared for the engines, oxygen equipment, structural members, wheels, fuel tanks, wiring, turrets, controls, instruments and the thousands of other parts of the airborne fighting machine. Often it meant working around the clock, without rest, to repair the damage of flak, rockets, machine-gun bullets and cannon shells. Behind each plane that flew to war was an army — mechanics, supply clerks, machinists, armorers, truck drivers, cooks — all the men who were just as vital to a successful mission as the pilots and their crews.

When a ship went down, each man died a little

The men who cared for the big bombers and stayed behind when the formations thundered into the east were closer to the air war over Europe than we could understand. The ground crews knew every square inch of their metal charges, worked on their airplanes with as much care as if they personally would meet the German flak and fighters. No ground crew ever really relaxed while the broad fields were emptied of the Liberators and Fortresses. The men shuffled about restlessly, worrying about manifold pressures and inches of mercury, how number four engine was holding up, whether the electrical system was okay in the ball turret, whether the thousand and one things they were responsible for would function when needed in temperatures sixty below zero. To the men on the ground, their bombers were almost living things, the air crews were their close friends. When a ship didn't come home, each man on the ground died a little.

Liberator flight engineer works closely with line chief to keep bomber in top operating condition *(above)*. Cold, grimy and weary (below), B-17 armorer prepares for long job of loading bombs.

Some of the men who stopped German bullets or flak high over Europe were lucky — they came home to England, as did this Fortress crew member, receiving plasma beneath his airplane. At times bombers returned with every man hit, several dead.

This is the side of the air war which received little attention — the wounded who returned to their bases crippled or blinded by flak, as is this B-17 crewman. A single raid over heavily defended targets sometimes cost as many as a thousand men killed, shot down, wounded, or suffering from frozen limbs. Flying and fighting 4 to 5 miles above the earth meant spending hours in exposed positions in temperatures down to 60° below zero, and the loss of limbs from the bitter cold by crewmen during fury of air fighting was suffered by many men.

A blinding flash: eleven men were dead

There were other dangers in maintaining a constant air campaign besides those which were found at 25,000 feet. Over England there was always the problem of holding formations in fog and clouds which rolled in suddenly and blanketed dozens of airfields in its sight-robbing mass; many men are no longer alive because their giant bombers met in mid-air and exploded. . . .

Sometimes accidents on the ground proved unavoidable. With the hundreds of thousands of heavy bombs which were uncrated, transported, fuzed and loaded aboard the big bombers, it was inevitable that there would be an accidental jarring of an arming device, a faulty fuze, an unexpected explosion . . . the shattered remains (in the *above* picture) are those of a Flying Fortress which suffered exactly that fate. Another B-17 stood on the runway, preparing to move into take-off position when, suddenly, there was a blinding flash, two and a half tons of bombs tore the heart out of the airplane . . . in a snap of the fingers, eleven men were dead. This B-17, Number Two in the line, went next. There were more. But the other planes moved out and took off to meet the German flak and fighters.

Mainstay of the Luftwaffe—the Messerschmitt Me-109G. Heavily armed, swift, maneuverable, it was one of the world's best fighters.

Its wing sheared off by flak, flaming B-17 of 452nd Bomb Group tumbles earthward over Chateaudun, France. Wild spin and gyrations during the plunge trapped crew; no parachutes were seen.

No other picture of the European air war so vividly portrays the terrible suddenness of fiery death in the air as this shot of a 465th Bomb Group, 15th AF Liberator, which caught a heavy flak bolt directly in its wing tanks. Spun upside down by blast, plane's tanks have exploded, and cracked fuselage in two. Note bombs tumbling from bays. A hit like this meant quick, flaming death.

They were lucky in this blazing Liberator. German fighters caught the B-24 in cross fire, set aflame the left inboard engine and wing tanks. In the few seconds available, nine men abandoned their stricken plane. Several seconds later, the left wing ripped loose.

Flushed with victory . . . faces of the enemy. Young pilots, gifted and skillful, courageous in the air. Our bomber crews will testify to that. These Messerschmitt pilots have just returned from a mission during which they shot down five Liberators, sent fifty American crewmen down to earth to die in flames, or to be captured. They often braved own flak to attack our planes.

Death in the air war wasn't always quick or clean — the last few seconds of this B-24, two thirds wrapped in flame, meant burning alive for its hapless crew. Moments later the bomber exploded.

Inside the cockpit of this burning B-17 a pilot braved the flames to keep the bomber on a level keel until his crew could safely abandon crippled Flying Fortress; all men bailed out of this ship.

The air war we never see. A dead B-17 gunner lies in German territory alongside the shattered hulk of his heavy bomber.

Four 1,000-lb. bombs begin their long trip down *(left)* to German targets in France. 9th AF medium bombers like the B-26 Marauders *(right)* carried out an unremitting aerial assault against enemy installations in occupied countries. Bombing from medium altitudes, Marauders, Havocs, Mitchells and Invaders smashed factories, docks, airfields, bridges, rail yards and lines. German flak was deadliest enemy of these bombers— their medium altitude runs were made to order for heavy 88-mm and lighter guns.

Ideally suited for desert operations, North American B-25 Mitchells hold formation at low altitude as they head for Tunisia. Ability of Mitchell to operate despite difficulties of primitive maintenance made it best AAF desert bomber. Major policy change in use of airpower was accomplished during North African campaign. After disaster at Kasserine Pass, control of AAF units was taken from local combat ground commands, passed on to theater commander who used planes to best advantage over entire front.

War of the mediums: Originally a mixed bomber and fighter organization whose B-24s, along with 8th AF Liberators, struck Ploesti in 1943, the 9th Air Force was rebuilt in October of that year in England as a tactical bomber outfit. For several months its medium bombers hammered at German aircraft and other factories, ports, robot bomb targets, airfields and railways. After D-Day the 9th's planes turned to a maximum air-ground co-operation effort, and cleared the way for our troops.

Launched on February 18, 1944, to choke off all communications to Anzio and Cassino fronts in Italy, Operation Strangle proved tremendous success. Direct hit *(below)* caught a train on rail bridge near Ficulle. Bridges, rails, roads were hammered daily. German supply convoys were decimated, isolating battlefront.

Douglas A-20 Havocs shower 500-lb. bombs on V-1 pilotless bomber sites in the Pas De Calais area in France *(above)*. Attacks against launching sites wasted more bombs than AAF dropped in all its raids against the Japanese homeland, proved ineffective in stopping the launchings. Low on fuel, its radio shot out, this B-26 *(below)* was guided back to its airfield in France by searchlight beams. The plane's luck held; this was its 164th combat mission.

For months preceding the all-out invasion of Europe on June 6, 1944, Allied airpower pounded German defenses in a day-and-night campaign which began to split the enemy's military force at the seams. The constant bombing by mediums (sometimes the price was high; *above*) of German rail lines and marshalling yards prevented needed supplies from reaching coastal defense positions; bombers also destroyed thousands of existing fortifications. In Italy the medium bomber and fighter-bomber proved highly effective in tying down the German army — with its thousands of tanks and mechanized vehicles, and several infantry divisions. After the inva-

sion, the Italian war was a forgotten conflict — overshadowed by the major fighting in France and Germany; it nevertheless played a vital role in the war by keeping powerful German forces bottled up in the peninsula. For the troops who had to climb their way over steep mountains, through thick mud, and across raging rivers and streams it was bitter fighting. Tactical airpower did a tremendous job of supporting our forces by destroying the enemy's effectiveness. A German general staff officer remarked sourly, "If we had the Allied Air Force which was in Italy, for one week, we would be back in Sicily at the end of that week."

Ghost tracks in the sky mark Thunderbolts diving for enemy fighters.

The long-range killers

Never during the great air battles over Europe did there arise any question as to the superiority of the three American fighters which met the best of the Luftwaffe in air-to-air combat, and decisively destroyed the opposition. The trio included the big twin-boomed Lightning; the sturdy, deep-chested Thunderbolt; and the swift and maneuverable Mustang. These were the fighters which outfought the Messerschmitts, Focke-Wulfs, Heinkels and Junkers. Not only did their performance enable them to fight from sea level to eight miles above the earth, but their extreme range meant that they could carry the fight to any place where the Germans might choose to make a stand. This point especially is most significant. Carrying their tremendous fuel and ammunition loads, the AAF fighters met German planes which were kept to a minimum weight, which fought under ideal defensive conditions, and whose pilots could almost always abandon their planes over friendly territory. It is interesting to note that the German air industry, unable to build a long-range fighter like the AAF big three, considered the task impossible. Unhampered by such thinking, American industry did the impossible. Further, not only were the P-38, P-47 and P-51 outstanding in air fighting, but they proved themselves conclusively the best fighter-bombers in the world.

Lockheed P-38 Lightning at 8th Air Force base in England *(right)* the evening before an escort mission to Germany. Flying since 1939, P-38 was first superior AAF fighter to reach ETO. A big, heavy airplane, it was also the first AAF fighter to escort bombers as far as Berlin. Badly needed in Pacific theater, Lightnings in 1944 and 1945 gave way to P-51, best ETO long-range escort.

A P-51 crew chief sweats out test hop of his Mustang, attached to 375th Fighter Squadron, 361st Fighter Group. Originally designed as a low-altitude support fighter, late-model P-51s used British-designed engine to improve high-altitude performance. Fastest single-engine fighter in Europe, it outclimbed, outmaneuvered German fighters. Germans considered it deadliest foe.

High over Flying Fortresses of the 15th Air Force, Lockheed Lightnings *(below)* leave twin vapor trails as they weave protectively over the big bombers. Twin engines of P-38 provided extra safety margin; with airplane's ability to absorb enemy fire and still fly, it brought many "dead men" home.

For the first time in seven hours — one long-range bomber escort mission — fighter pilot Lt. Vernon R. Richards *(left)* can relax. Note mission co-ordinates inked on hand. Thunderbolt fighter *(above)*, belly tank jettisoned, races toward enemy fighters.

With belly tanks trailing great sheets of flame, the pilot of this stricken Me-109G fighter *(below)* managed to jettison the burning tanks, escaped by crashing in heavy snow.

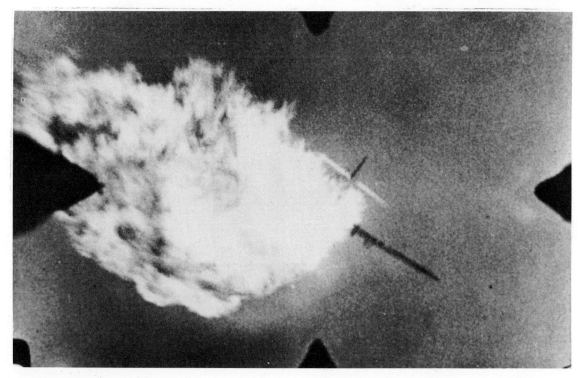

American infantryman stands perimeter guard at forward airfield in Normandy *(above)* after invasion of France. Picture dramatizes the close co-operation between ground forces and 9th AF's fighter-bombers, which afforded our troops and armored units unprecedented striking power. Carrying up to two tons of bombs. Thunderbolts tore German communications to ribbons, killed and wounded thousands of soldiers, collapsed bridges, cut rail lines, and effectively isolated the forward battlefield from reinforcements.

Ninth Air Force Thunderbolts caught this locomotive in the middle of a 300-foot span across the Moselle River, and wrecked both the bridge and engine with precision dive bombing. Freight cars in the background were then strafed and set ablaze. Several thousand tons of vitally needed supplies in this one train alone never reached desperate German troops, who soon ran low on food, fuel, ammunition, medical and other supplies. Cut off, many German units had to abandon their frontline positions.

Ninth Air Force pilots report successes and events of their missions to intelligence officer at home base. Claims of pilots were checked carefully to determine actual value of missions, and automatic gun cameras often recorded details missed by pilots flying at high speed close to the ground. Experiences of the fighter-bomber pilots at times seemed impossible. One 15th Air Force P-38 was strafing a German ammunition truck at treetop level when the vehicle exploded violently. The explosion, through which the Lightning had to fly, knocked out its right engine, blew pieces of Nazi uniforms, shell casings, and even some empty German cigarette packages into the dazed pilot's air scoop. Thunderbolts often came back to their fields riddled with hundreds of bullet and cannon holes, looking like flying sieves. Next day the rugged planes went out again.

Two heavy bombs fall away from diving Thunderbolt; Bologna, Italy.

Republic P-47 Thunderbolt pilots of the 57th Fighter Group in Italy used a new trick to get at German troops. Strafing runs sent Germans scurrying inside barns, farmhouses, and other structures in assembly area near Pavulla, along the Fifth Army front. Pilots dove to low altitudes, jettisoned their external fuel tanks, drenching the buildings. Repeated strafing runs with incendiary bullets set gasoline aflame, engulfing buildings and vital materials stored within in searing fire. Interdiction effort in Italy was made to order for fighter-bombers like P-47s and the big P-38s; narrow mountain passes, high railway bridges and long, narrow roads were cut repeatedly. Major effort in Mediterranean also was made against German shipping. Fighters roamed coastlines, shooting up and bombing the hundreds of small vessels enemy used to carry vital supplies.

123

Airborne and unarmed

No single air operation before or since has ever matched the tremendous power assembled, or the co-ordination achieved, during the invasion of France on June 6, 1944. Especially — hazardous — was the vertical attack behind German lines; to drop 17,000 men from the sky, the AAF staged the greatest troop carrier operation ever known. Long sky trains which included 900 transport planes and more than 100 gliders lifted the 17,000 men

Douglas C-47 of the 9th Troop Carrier Command carrying paratroopers *(above)* to drop zone during invasion of Holland, September 17, 1944. CG-4A gliders *(below)* landed engineers in open fields, permitting building airfields during the fighting.

Waves of paratroopers drop near Crave, reinforcing units which had jumped earlier.

and all their equipment. The attack was fraught with great risk, and in the initial drops made in darkness there was much confusion and error. Thousands of men landed in the thick of powerful German forces; others were scattered over marshes and fields and so were ineffective. Much of this was due to violent enemy resistance, and German flak, machine-gun and light-arms fire took a terrible toll of the unarmed transports (*above, center*) and the gliders: 42 transport planes and 9 gliders were blown out of the air. Despite their difficulties, the airborne did a valuable job. Army staff officers stated that "the success of the Utah (beachhead) assault could not have been achieved so conspicuously without the work of the airborne forces."

There were more vertical envelopments to come. In mid-September, 2,800 planes and 1,600 gliders landed an entire airborne army in Holland. On March 24, 1945, 3,000 transports and gliders moved more than 40,000 men from France and England to the east bank of the Rhine River.

Rigged for jumping, heavily armed, and with faces blackened, these paratroopers assist each other in fastening their chutes. Two divisions of paratroopers and glider troops hit behind the German lines on the opening day of the invasion, as other men fought to break through German defenses along the Normandy beaches. It was one of war's roughest jobs; casualties were high.

ANOTHER WORLD, ANOTHER AIR WAR

Mediums, fighters bore brunt of heavy fighting

The long return to Japan was sparked in the southwest Pacific by a major land and air push within New Guinea, and the triphibious assault against Guadalcanal and other Solomon Islands. The fight to retake major installations on New Guinea included an incredibly difficult airlift over the Own Stanley Mountains to near Buna; planes were so short in supply that B-17s ferried artillery. On January 2, 1943, the Buna airfield was overrun, and the threat to the vital Port Moresby airfield complex eliminated. In the late summer of 1942 AAF planes hit Japanese positions on Guadalcanal, Tulagi, New Guinea, and Rabaul, while Navy and Marine fliers stormed up and down the Solomons, raising havoc with Jap shipping and airfields. On August 7, 1942, the Marines went ashore on Guadalcanal, and for three critical months waged a bloody war with the enemy. By late October we had built up AAF-USN-USMC air superiority, and one month later AAF heavy bombers operated from Henderson Field on Guadalcanal. This was only the first step toward Rabaul, and it was followed by invasion of the New Georgia islands in the central Solomons at the end of June, 1943, and by invasion of Bougainville in late November.

Lightnings on patrol. High speed, excellent rate of climb, long range, altitude performance, heavy firepower and especially its tremendous diving speed made P-38 the most feared and hated AAF fighter plane in all Pacific, according to Japanese pilots.

No one airplane hurt the Japanese in the southwest Pacific more than the B-25, flown by its pilots under every conceivable combat condition. Here a Mitchell screams low over burning Jap freighter at Rabaul, while piers blaze fiercely from earlier bombing, strafings.

Mediums hammered all targets

A high-ranking Japanese officer, who survived AAF attacks against his airfields on New Guinea and New Ireland islands, reported after the war: "The American medium bomber pilots who raided our fields were the wildest fliers I have ever encountered. They were also some of the bravest. They would stop at nothing; they flew at treetop level, racing at great speed over our fields, their machine guns spraying lead and tracers into every possible target." The enemy description is accurate. Nowhere else on all the AAF's fighting fronts were our pilots more daring or skillful than in their minimum-level assaults on Japanese airfields, ships, installations, bridges and railways, across the Pacific and in Asia (above; bridge-busting in China). Clipping masts on ships or returning to base with bamboo stuck in air intakes was a common occurrence; pilots beat up enemy targets at altitudes from as low as ten feet, seldom over several hundred. Field modifications turned lightly armed bombers into virtual flying arsenals.

A-20 roars low over Japanese airfield on Lae, New Guinea, strafing planes, men and anything which resembles a worth-while target. Treetop attacks crippled airfields.

Wreckage of Japanese Zero fighters at Lae airfield testifies to effectiveness of AAF medium and light bomber attacks. Our planes struck in day and night raids, often brushing treetops to pour in demolition and phosphorus bombs and parafrags.

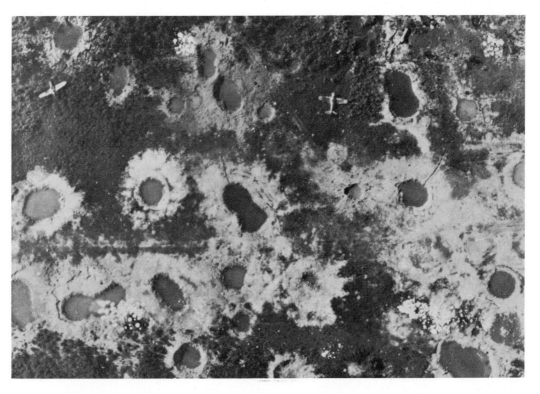

Two wrecked Japanese fighters are surrounded by giant, water-filled craters punched by heavy bombs in enemy airfield at Gasmata, New Britain, by AAF and Australian planes. The runway is totally useless despite constant repairs by the Japanese, who lost the use of their fields on islands in the Southwest Pacific through similar damage.

Japanese shipping took terrific beating

The AAF's pilots, especially those of the 5th Air Force, threw away the rulebook when they went after enemy warships and merchantmen in the Pacific and in Asia. Armorers ripped bombsights and other equipment from the noses of medium and light bombers, piled in up to eight heavy machine guns; they also bolted as many as four guns to fuselages. Thus a B-25 making a low-level strike at a ship could rake the vessel's gunners with as many as twelve fixed .50-caliber guns, plus fire from turrets. This was enough of a blow in itself to sink small freighters and warships. The most spectacular means of attack, however, was skip-bombing. Bombers raced in at low height, dropped their bombs when still flying straight and level. They could heave their bombs directly into a ship's side or, by modifying the approach run, could skip the bombs along the water until they crashed into the thin hulls of their targets.

Now you see it . . .

. . . now you don't! Photographer aboard B-25 formation attacking Japanese corvette off Rabaul harbor caught this picture sequence. In top picture, corvette starts to swerve in attempt to escape stick of bombs approaching ship. Bottom pictures tells its own story. Direct hit with 500-lb. bomb tore corvette into wreckage which sank at once.

It's anybody's guess as to how this skip-bombing Havoc (below) missed this freighter's mast. Two planes each sent two 500-lb. bombs into ship's side, blowing the hull open.

Medium and light bombers were favored targets of Japanese fighters. Flying at low altitude, unescorted on most of their missions, the mediums were fair game as they roared in at zero heights to hit sea and land targets. Japanese Army Oscar fighter swings against evading Mitchell over Hansa Bay, New Guinea as bomber pulls away from run over enemy shipping. Oscar made long curving pass at B-25, was caught in fire from bomber's turret. Both planes escaped with light damage. Bomber pilots tried to catch fighters in heavy forward firepower.

Outstanding pilot skill of men who flew B-25s against shipping is evident in this picture of Mitchell which barely scraped over mast of Japanese picket boat. Caught by bombers off the coast of Paramushiru, in the Kurile Islands, this and other picket boats were strafed to kill deck gunners, hit with depth-bomb salvos which sank ships.

Japanese went to desperate measures to conceal their merchant ships and cargo-carrying barges from low-flying AAF and Australian fighters and bombers. Draped with jungle vines and leaves, this oil-carrying barge was caught by RAAF Beaufighter, strafed with cannon shells which exploded oil drums and gutted the vessel.

"You are out to kill"...

On the first of March, 1943, a patrolling B-24 spotted a Japanese convoy of nine merchant ships and eight destroyers steaming off the northern coast of New Britain. The next morning B-17s and B-24s with P-38 escorts sank or damaged four ships. On March 3rd, the 5th AF unleashed a thunderbolt against the convoy as it sailed into Huon Gulf. Beaufighters went in first to kill off the AA crews. Heavy bombers released salvos from medium altitude, diverting attention from fast, low-flying A-20s and B-25s which poured bursts of .50-caliber fire into the ships and then skipped their bombs into the vessels. Other planes hammered nearby airfields, and P-38s disposed of the Jap fighters trying to protect the convoy. When it was over, only four battered destroyers escaped. The next day A-20s and Beaufighters strafed survivors in the water who were trying to reach the main Japanese forces on nearby islands. An AAF officer said, "This was the dirty part of the job...some of the boys got sick. But...you are out to kill the enemy."

Skip-bombing B-25s confused Japanese, who thought planes were making torpedo runs (above). Note bomb skipping off water.

Cargo ship used as troop transport trails blazing oil on water. Every single one of nine merchant ships in convoy went to bottom.

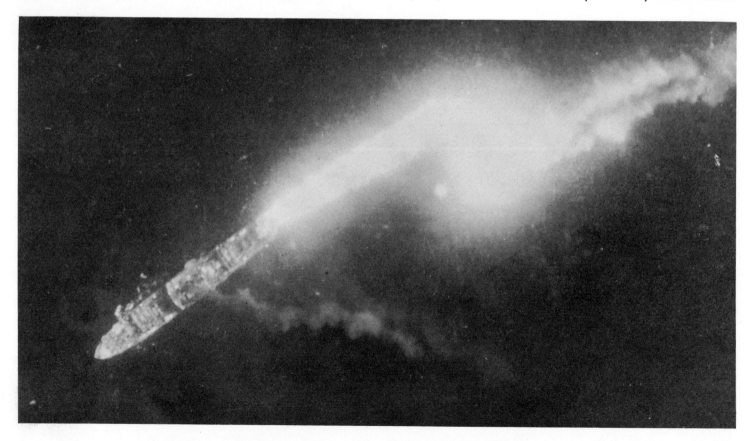

Mitchell bomber flies low over the desolate frozen wasteland of Shimushu, the northernmost island in the Kuriles chain, to strike at convoy in Paramushiru Strait. War in frozen north meant long missions, fighting violent weather and enemy, little recognition.

Canneries and Zeros

On October 6, 1943, the Eleventh Air Force received warning that an air assault on Attu Island was imminent. One week later ten Japanese bombers flew with impunity high over American P-40s, dropped their bombs wastefully in open fields, and fled. It was the last enemy attack of the war in the Aleutians.

American activity against the enemy in the Kuriles was barely more energetic. After a severe mauling by Japanese flak and fighters on September 11, 1943, operations in the dismal northland diminished steadily. Infrequent attacks were made against Kuriles shipping, airfields, fisheries and canneries. By mid-1944 most of the 11th Air Force personnel in the Aleutians were transferred elsewhere, and bases east of Adak were reduced to the status of gasoline stations. Only 39 bombers and one squadron of fighters remained in the islands.

Bombers which flew to Kuriles from their Aleutians bases never knew when home fields would be socked in on return flights; these Liberators just made it in as snowstorm enveloped base, closed down runways.

Liberators fly high, far

Bombs spill from bays of a Convair B-24 Liberator *(above)* over Wake Island, April, 1944. Long range made B-24 Pacific favorite. Japanese resorted to wide variety of air weapons against AAF heavy bombers, like this streaming aerial phosphorous bomb *(below)* which exploded in midst of Liberator formation during attack against Truk Island. The phosphorous bombs were rarely effective.

This is probably the most accurate bombing ever achieved during the entire war. From 14,000 feet a B-24 Liberator of the 308th Bomb Group, 14th Air Force, dropped a heavy bomb perfectly on a hairline, 10-foot wide target — the "Old Yellow River Bridge," China's longest river structure. No pilot would believe it — but here's the proof.

Machines, blood, oil on world's biggest airline

At the peak of its wartime operations the AAF's Air Transport Command sent an airplane on an Atlantic crossing once every thirteen minutes; across the expansive Pacific, once every ninety minutes. Every part of the globe became home to the big ATC airliners, which made routine the flights over oceans, mountains and vast uninhabited areas which would have been considered impossible in prewar days. ATC pilots flew combat planes as well, ferrying fighters and bombers to forward battle areas. The goods carried by this global air network ranged anywhere from diamonds of pinhead size to giant road-building machinery. Ammunition, ping-pong balls, whole blood, trucks, bombs, gasoline, oil, food, animals — whatever was needed, the Army's airline flew. No other operation, however, could compare with the spine-chilling flights across the towering Himalayas in Asia. To support the 14th Air Force and the B-29s of the XX Bomber Command, ATC carried the fuel, bombs, trucks and other supplies needed to sustain these fighting groups. Flying over the highest mountains in the world, taking their chances with fighters in their unarmed transports, ATC's pilots carved their niche in the AAF's history.

Careful maneuvering, a keen eye, and plenty of muscle were required to load this 5,250-lb. weapons-carrier vehicle into a Curtiss C-46 Commando transport, for flight across towering Himalaya peaks (*top picture*). In July, 1945, ATC hit a record in its flying operations, averaged one flight over the forbidding Hump every 1.3 minutes. In one year, ATC flew 500,000 tons of war supplies and personnel around the world.

A Curtiss C-46 Commando of the Fourteenth Air Force comes in for a landing at an AAF airfield in China. Commandos were biggest twin-engine transports of the war, carried vehicles weighing up to thirteen tons on high-altitude flights. Many of the pilots flying ATC planes were civilian airline fliers who were commissioned as officers, flew commercial planes under military control. In 1945, ATC was 200,000 members strong.

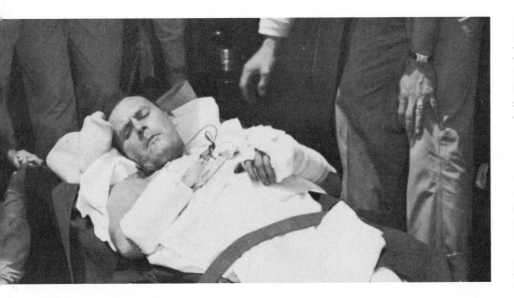

His right arm amputated, and his left limb badly shot up, Captain Edward J. Berry was one of many combat wounded the Air Transport Command rushed back to the United States from the Pacific and the European theaters for the care available in stateside hospitals. Quick evacuation is credited with saving thousands of lives.

The evacuation of combat wounded from the front lines to rear-area hospitals, or directly to the United States, often was a grim race with death. The critically wounded soldier *(below)* weakened seriously during his evacuation flight aboard a hospital plane. Corpsman and nurse pulled him through with emergency blood transfusion.

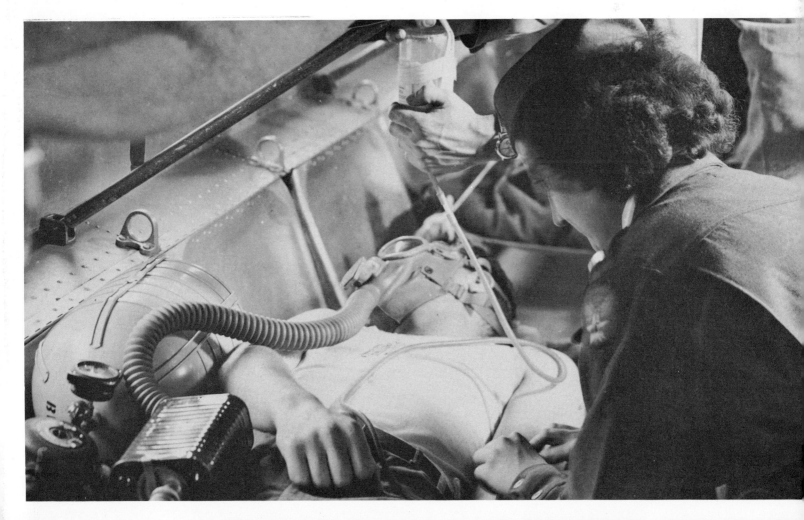

7-league boots fighters

With the debut of the P-38 in the Southwest Pacific, AAF hopes to whip Japan's agile fighters soared. P-38 pilots made sure not to commit the error of trying to dog-fight with the maneuverable Zeros — the most nimble fighters in the world. Carefully employing their airplane's superior characteristics, Lightning pilots adopted the hard rule of *never* attempting to turn with a Zero. Able to climb and to outdive the Zero, with greater endurance and range, P-38s used to advantage their superior fire-power and higher ceiling. They chose combat where and when it was most promising — with results devastating to the enemy. High-flying P-38s dove on Zeros, scattered the Japanese fighters — right into the guns of lower-flying P-39s and P-40s. Lightning pilots led the AAF's aces. Bong scored 40 confirmed air kills, McGuire 38, to become two top AAF aces, and of the ten leading pilots in World War II, four flew the big twin-boomed P-38. Like Dick Bong, many of them owed their lives to Lightning's rugged ability to bring them home on one engine.

Lightnings climb out from take-off at Tacloban Field on Leyte, Philippines. P-38 was the number one air killer in the Pacific.

Lt. Richard Ira Bong in cockpit of his P-38 Lightning fighter, March 6th, 1943, in New Guinea. Assigned to 49th Fighter Group, Fifth Air Force, Bond used superior performance of P-38 to score 40 air kills. Several times he lost one engine, beat out pursuing Zero fighters. On August 5, 1945, Bong took off from Burbank, Calif., in new jet fighter, was killed when plane exploded.

Why pilots loved the Lightning. During a strike against Iwo Jima, this 7th Air Force P-38 limped away from the target with its left engine shot out (note feathered prop), a gaping hole torn in the right wing, which is in flames. Pilot nursed his crippled ship back to Saipan in 4-hour, 40-minute grueling overwater flight for a distance which was greater than that from London to Berlin.

Asian air commandos and mud on Guadalcanal

The Tenth and Fourteenth Air Forces which fought along a 6,000-mile front in China and southern Asian countries were formed from a varied assortment of special air task forces and the remnants of the old Flying Tigers. Despite their serious supply problems in so remote an area, the B-25s, P-40s and P-51s wreaked havoc on the enemy, strafing and killing thousands of their troops, shooting up communications, cutting bridges and rail lines. Even the B-24 pilots forgot about the restrictions of their planes and brought their big bombers down to treetop level. The air effort in the Solomons represented the combined force of the AAF, Navy and Marines. For a while crowded Henderson Field on Guadalcanal had more of a problem from local air traffic than it did from the enemy.

Primitive conditions under which mechanics operated at Guadalcanal airfields *(below)* is well illustrated in this picture of crude wooden pole hoist being used to lift Bell P-39 Airacobra off ground for servicing. Planes flew against enemy from worst airfield conditions; often maintenance was carried out with improvised equipment and more ingenuity than spare parts. Here Airacobra proved its worth; designed specifically for maintenance under rough field conditions, it was well suited to jungle operations.

Colonel Philip Cochran, Mustang fighter pilot in First Air Commando Force, ready for sweep mission against Japanese in Burma.

U.S.S. _Manila Bay_ slips past water geysers from bomb explosions as Japanese planes attack during fighting for Saipan, June, 1944. Thunderbolts were catapulted off carrier, landed on Saipan.

With whirling P-47 propellers barely ten feet over his head, T/5 James B. Lazar worries only about road traffic crossing the runway. Thunderbolts flew from Saipan to work over Iwo Jima.

The vast, lonely sea

Unlike pilots in the ETO, those who bailed out over the vast stretches of the Pacific could not look forward to survival even as prisoners. With a special hatred for fliers, Japanese troops seldom allowed downed pilots to live very long, and there was little choice about gambling upon the ocean. But thanks to a far-flung air-sea rescue organization, thousands of men who bailed out into the ocean lived to fight another day — like this jubilant Australian fighter pilot who waves his arms wildly to circling AAF OA-10 flying boat. He was incredibly lucky; he had no signaling devices, but his raft was spotted by alert observer. Navy PBY *(right)* approaches Hermit Island to pick up bomber crew after their plane had crashed on beach.

The beginning of the end

The early days of the strategic bomber campaign to burn Japan out of the war were easily some of the most frustrating in all Air Force history. The B-29 itself was new, temperamental, full of engineering "bugs," which only time and continued engineering could eliminate. Worst of all was the air base and supply problem in Asia; in January, 1944, Brigadier General K. B. Wolfe flew to India to check on progress at rear bases. "We wanted runways," said Wolfe. "We found a bunch of Indians making mud pies." An appeal to the Army for help produced a miracle. General Joe Stilwell, local Army commander, pulled his Negro engineers off the Ledo Road and they "came with a battery of concrete mixers, and put on the damndest exhibition of concrete laying you ever saw," General Wolfe recalls. In China the problems were magnified by the requirements for a major air-base

network. Somehow, the fields were built. But it was a backbreaking way to fight a war, let alone realize the kind of campaign that visionary air planners desired. In addition to supplies flown in by ATC, the B-29s freighted their own essentials to forward China bases — gasoline, spare parts, engines, food, ammunition, tools, hangar equipment, clothing, medicine, oil, bombs. For every combat mission, each B-29 had to make six 1,000-mile flights over the towering Hump. The first attack of the war saw 98 B-29s take off from India bases the morning of June 5, 1944, to bomb the Makasan railroad shops at Bangkok. Two minutes after take-off, one plane crashed and killed 10 of the 11 men aboard. Twelve more B-29s aborted the raid because of mechanical and other difficulties. The remaining planes bombed their target, then were caught in a 100-mph gale of yellow-purple clouds which scattered 30 bombers over China. But on June 15, 1944 — the day Saipan was invaded — a B-29 force struck at Yawata, Japan. Damage was slight. But for the Japanese it was a disaster — it was the beginning of the end.

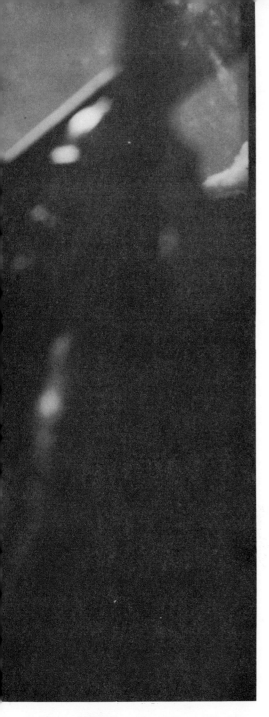

During operations from bases in China and India, B-29s often found storms a more dangerous enemy than Japanese fighter planes. Bombardier *(above)* in nose scans the China skies for enemy planes as B-29, high over solid overcast, heads for Formosa. In October, 1944, three missions against the island bastion, involving 198 B-29s, virtually demolished the great Okayama airplane assembly plant with more than 1,200 tons of bombs. Japanese attempts to send aerial reinforcements to Philippines were hampered by B-29 and carrier strikes against Formosa.

Superfortresses high over China on their way to Japan. The B-29's gunnery system, which used central sighting systems and remote control turrets, exceeded all expectations in combat. On a lone photographic mission, a Superfortress was jumped by 90 enemy fighters over Japan. For more than an hour the harried plane fought off fierce attacks. Confused by the B-29's high speed and great operating altitude, seven fighters went down in flames as the big American bomber fled, undamaged. The bombardier on the B-29 *Pioneer III,* Lt. Jack T. Hull was in the airplane's nose during a mission over Singapore. Explosion of an AA shell destroyed Hull's right eye, severely injured his right hand and arm. Hull slipped on an oxygen mask without telling the crew of his injuries, salvoed his bombs on signal, closed the bomb doors, waiting until the formation was out of the target run. Only then, drenched with blood, did he call for help.

AAF BECOMES SUPR

Army Air Force is now most powerful military force in history. Germany pounded from air, by land into submission. Japan's cities gutted—AAF changes history: victory without invasion

A matter for the record

By the close of 1944 the Army Air Force stood as the most powerful military force in history. Its planes were sweeping aside the desperate air defenses of Germany, and reducing that nation's once-proud industry to ash and rubble. In the air the cream of the Luftwaffe rose in final gasps which hurled thousands of planes at our fighters and bombers — only to have even these frenzied attempts crushed beneath an American air armada which never faltered in its devastating air campaign. At war's end a wealth of testimony from German officials conceded that strategic bombing had broken the back of the German war machine and stripped the German army of the strength and mobility with which it had hoped to throw us off the continent. German generals emphasized with justifiable bitterness that had the Allied armies not enjoyed such tremendous power in the skies, the Normandy invasion would have been transformed into a gigantic blood bath. The air campaign against Germany's fuel industry reached its peak in February, 1945, when *all* German gasoline refineries were either bombed out or shut down. The roads of Europe were cluttered with undamaged German armor which lacked even the gasoline to flee before our advancing ground forces. All across Europe, German trains and road columns stalled helplessly because our planes had smashed bridges, closed tunnels and ripped road and rail systems to shreds. Much of this aerial effort went unseen by the American infantryman, and it was difficult to impress upon him that such activity made his task that much easier. But he could see, and he certainly understood, the sight of thousands of German troops who had been sent into shock by the terrible impact of carpet bombing. A German war correspondent reported to his people that "the front lines could not hold out because the Allies bombed sector after sector, laid their carpet of bombs and decimated one unit after the other before the real attack began. The effect on the morale of German troops . . . was disastrous . . ."

After the victory was gained critics rose to point out that Germany, despite its defeat, led the world in aeronautical science, that it was the AAF who trailed the enemy. This was less than half the story, however, for the noteworthy German scientific accomplishments all were admissions of defeat. They were measures of desperation aimed at destroying our air force — necessary because the German air force had failed to do so. German air science, despite its dazzling toys, failed to meet the acid test: it could not produce the weapons to win the air battle and, consequently, the war.

Student bombardiers prepare for night mission in Beech trainer. AAF's combat units in entire war dropped 2,057,000 tons of bombs on enemy targets — three fourths of it against Germany. A total of 1,693,000 combat missions were flown in Europe.

145

Rampaging fighters smashed Luftwaffe

There was never a brighter day among the AAF pilots in Europe than when orders from headquarters "took the overalls off" our fighter planes. The news that fighters could break away from their high-altitude escort positions, and were permitted to go after the German air force in the air and on the ground, meant a promise of unprecedented aerial victories and destruction by strafing. As many as two thousand fighters in one day ranged over Europe in gangs, spoiling for trouble. Anything with a black cross was fair game, and our fighters plunged from high altitude in a wild free-for-all after any and all opposition. The three 15th A.F. Mustangs *(above),* peeling off from bomber escort, belonged to the 31st Fighter Group; with 570 enemy planes destroyed in aerial combat; it finally had to turn to strafing runs to find worthwhile targets. Over Germany especially did the fighter sweeps produce lucrative results. Hundreds of our planes roared low over the land, seeking targets of opportunity and burning planes on the ground (Nordhausen airfield, February, 1945; *below).*

Engine blazing, FW-190 is helpless before AAF fighter.

Two Thunderbolt pilots teamed up to write *finis* to this twin-engined Messerschmitt Me-110 fighter. One P-47 had ripped open Me-100's left wing (note burning fuel tank) when second Thunderbolt raced in, cut in front of first P-47, and quickly finished the job.

German pilot tumbles through the air as he abandons his shot-up Focke-Wulf FW-190 fighter. German ship jumped a dive-bombing P-47; latter released his heavy missiles, pulled around in climbing turn. Thunderbolt's heavy machine guns tore the FW-190 apart.

This Messerschmitt Me-109G fighter, its right wing tank exploding, was climbing after an AAF fighter and firing its three cannon when a second AAF plane came in from behind, exploded the wing tank, and blew the entire wing off the airplane. Both the Focke-Wulf FW-190 and Messerschmitt Me-109G fighters were excellent, high-performance machines. However, despite their heavy weight of fuel and guns, AAF fighters consistently emerged the victor from the wild aerial melees over Germany.

Fighters paralyzed German communications

On the morning of February 22, 1945, the Allied air forces, with the AAF representing the bulk of strength in the air, flew Operation Clarion. Ten thousand planes went after more than 200 communications targets over an area of a quarter of a million square miles — with the express purpose of paralyzing the *Reichsban*. Planes operated in small units of squadrons and flights and fanned out over Germany. All across the country bombs exploded on mashalling yards, signal control points, main lines, level crossings, embankments, bridges, viaducts, roundhouses, overpasses and junctions. Fighters and fighter-bombers paid particular attention to rolling stock. Immediately, according to the German rail organization, war production was cut in half, and rail traffic was slashed by 90 per cent. From that day on, the mobility of the German army was a thing of the past. The fighters and fighter-bombers never slackened their assaults. Without respite they severed vital transportation arteries, collapsed bridges, shot up trains, turned rail lines into an endless succession of bomb craters. The German army finally had to travel almost entirely on foot.

Bridge to nowhere. German army relied upon rail bridges to move supplies to needed battlefronts. Fighter-bombers blew this bridge across Seine, isolated several trainloads of ammunition.

Hundreds of railroad cars, many of them loaded with ammunition and military supplies, were destroyed in devastating attack against rail marshalling yards at Limburg, isolating front lines.

Jackknifed locomotive *(above)* at Muenster. Italy rail line *(below)*. **Terrific blast** of 1,000-lb. bomb hurled this locomotive into crater.

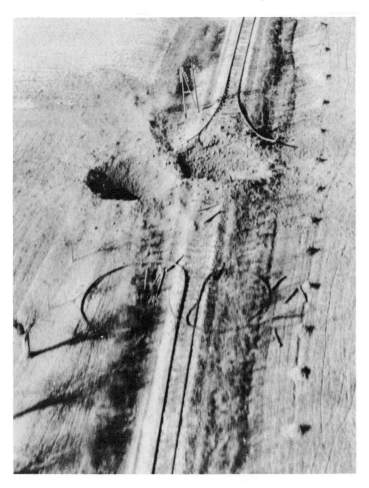

No respite from the air

On January 21, 1945, General-leutnant Fritz Bayerlein, commander of the crack Panzer Lehr Division, approached the Gemuend bridge near Aachen, where his forces were massing for an attack against advancing American units. The general, who was still a considerable distance from the actual fighting, was stunned by the sight which met his eyes. A vast swarm of American planes circled in the air, many of them swooping down to the earth in regular intervals, shooting almost without interruption. "I had to thread a way," the general said, "through wrecked and burning vehicles, dead horses, scattered equipment. It was a one-way bridge, and planes caught traffic on both sides. Several hundred vehicles were destroyed and the column thrown into panic."

The soldiers in the cart dead from strafing by P-47s, frenzied horse used for transport in Bologna, Italy, bolts wildly from road.

The Kaiserlautern-Bad Durkeim Road, Germany *(below).* Destroyed vehicles, dead soldiers and horses lined highway for miles.

With 25 planes to his credit, Capt. Robert S. Johnson had to turn to strafing to find targets for his Thunderbolt's heavy guns.

Strafing attacks against retreating German vehicles *(below)* on roads in the Vicenza, Italy, area killed and wounded thousands of enemy troops, turned the highways into certain deathtraps.

Medium bombers eased infantryman's task

Medium bombers like these Martin B-26 Marauders *(above)* which sometimes crossed the towering Alps to hammer at objectives in southwest Germany proved some of the best friends of the American infantry. After the European invasion, the twin-engine planes concentrated on hitting targets which would most benefit the infantry's task of pushing into Germany. During six days of the Battle of the Bulge, the 9th Air Force's 9th Bombardment Division alone made 1,300 combat sorties and dropped 2,500 tons of bombs on bridges, highway junctions, rail yards, gun positions, supply dumps and airfields. Supporting the First and Third Armies, the 9th Air Force on the red-letter day of December 26, 1944, knocked out 136 tanks and armored vehicles, 15 horse-drawn transports, 21 gun positions, 520 motor vehicles, damaged 100 rail cars, hit 10 rail passes and blew up three ammunition dumps.

The medium bombers were especially vulnerable to the massed antiaircraft weapons of German ground forces. At their bombing heights they could be hit both with the heavy 88-mm guns and lighter weapons, and sometimes the planes suffered severe losses in their attacks against heavily defended targets. This Douglas A-26 Invader, which had a wing blown off by the direct hit of a flak shell, was making a low-altitude run against German gun positions. Note bombs in racks. Hurtling earthward out of control, the A-26 was too low when hit for its crew to abandon the airplane — one of the grimmer aspects of medium-bomber warfare.

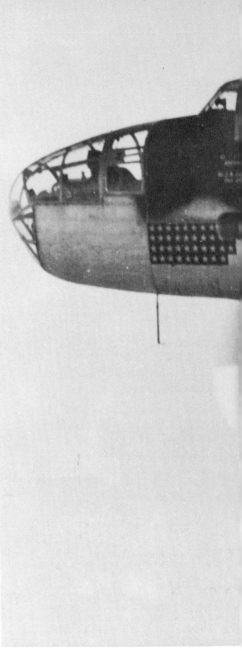

The last element of a 1st Tactical Air Force B-25 Mitchell medium-bomber formation passes over boiling smoke and dust from bombs which destroyed a rail and highway bridge at Pietrasanta, Italy.

To destroy vital rail links, viaducts and bridges, medium bombers flew tight formations, "walked" long strings of bombs across the target, destroying powerfully built rail and bridge installations and destroying the surrounding areas. An excellent example of the results of this type of attack is seen in this broken span of the Seefeld railroad bridge in Austria, hit by 15th Air Force mediums. In areas shown in this picture, heavy bombs cut the steel-and-concrete span in two places and cratered rail lines.

A string of 500-pounders drops away from a B-25 Mitchell of the 12th Air Force during an attack against the Roverto railroad bridge along the vital Brenner Pass. Enormous concentrations of bombs smashed rail lines, bridges, power stations, tunnel entrances and exits to create a bottleneck along these vital mountainous arteries between Germany and Italy. Operation Strangle cut off most of German army supplies.

Medium and light bombers of the Ninth Air Force proved their adaptability to forward field conditions by flying from emergency bases set up in France. An A-20 Havoc (right) of the 410th Bomb Group moves into take-off position over snow-packed airstrip for combat mission. Ground crews did a marvelous job of maintaining airplanes under primitive conditions, and they worked round the clock in bitter temperatures.

Martin Marauders trail weird wing-tip streamers as they fly over Alps *(above)*. Linz marshalling yards in Austria *(below)* are scene of utter destruction after heavy raids by 15th Air Force bombers.

It is aerodynamically impossible for this B-25, its nose shot off by flak, to fly. With bombardier and navigator blown into space, pilot flew wildly bucking airplane back to base; crew bailed out.

Douglas A-26 Invaders of the 9th Bombardment Division *(right)* return to their home field after leaving in flames a German ammunition dump near Rheinbach, ten miles southwest of Bonn. A late-comer to the European air war, the swift Invaders remained first-line bombers in USAF for years afterward, proved their worth in the Korean air fighting which began in June of 1950.

When this Douglas A-20G Havoc light bomber of the 9th USAAF *(right)* was hit by flak the explosion tore the tail section completely from the airplane. Note the plane's rudder flipping between the left engine and the fuselage. Other pieces of flak may be seen in the air. The Havoc whipped out of control, trapping the hapless crew inside. Havocs operated in ETO as medium bombers.

In February, 1945, 9th Air Force headquarters withdrew altitude restrictions from its medium bombers. A B-26 Marauder *(below)* which normally made its attacks at 10,000 to 13,000 feet, takes advantage of its new freedom to make a tree-top strafing and bombing run against a factory at Montabaur, Germany. New change in tactics caught enemy by surprise, allowed far deadlier accuracy to be achieved by the mediums which adopted fighter-bomber roles.

Defeat came from the skies

Wesel, Germany: It impeded infantry advance; AAF "removed it."

"Allied air power was decisive in the war in western Europe. Hindsight inevitably suggests that it might have been employed differently or better in some respects. Nevertheless, it was decisive. In the air, its victory was complete; at sea, its contribution, combined with naval power, brought an end to the enemy's greatest naval threat — the U-boat; on land, it helped turn the tide overwhelmingly in favor of Allied ground forces. Its power and superiority made possible the success of the invasion. It brought the economy which sustained the enemy's armed forces to virtual collapse, although the full effects of this collapse had not reached the enemy's front lines when they were overrun by Allied forces. It brought home to the German people the full impact of modern war with all its horror and suffering. Its imprint on the German nation will be lasting."

The United States Strategic Bombing Survey

Flak bursts spill through vapor trails of 97th Bomb Group (15th AF) Flying Fortresses as they move into their bomb runs over the rail yards at Graz, Austria. By March, 1945, the German rail system was virtually in collapse, and roads had become impassable.

Salvo of heavy bombs from Liberator *(right)* drops toward heavy clouds which cover German city. Great masses of clouds which blanketed Germany during last months of war required heavy use of radar-bombing techniques, which proved remarkably accurate. In June of 1944, AAF hurled 120,000 tons of bombs against German targets — compared to the less than 12,000 tons which the Luftwaffe achieved during its best month during height of the blitz against England. Germany was paralyzed by January, 1945; her ruin was an accomplished fact months before her troops quit.

Paving the way for a ground advance by a blistering bombardment of enemy positions directly in the path of our troops became an established AAF procedure in fight to destroy Germany. It was tried — and it failed — at Cassino. It succeeded brilliantly in Normandy preceding the St. Lo breakthrough. In mid-November of 1944 the Army called for complete obliteration of Düren *(left)*, a powerful strong point blocking its push toward Cologne. With 2,970 tons of bombs, RAF erased city's center. 8th AF sent 996 B-17s and 243 B-24s to drop additional 4,120 tons of heavy bombs.

Nazi best not enough

The strategic air destruction of the Third Reich was a two-pronged assault, with the RAF contributing its heaviest blows from 1943 on. With single raids of 4,899 tons of bombs, the RAF piled ruin upon ruin in German cities, immobolized millions of workers and severely disrupted economic life. For the AAF, 72 per cent of all bombs were dropped on German targets *after* July 1, 1944. It was this avalanche of explosives which broke the back of Germany's mighty industrial machine — a complex which was far more powerful than our intelligence had originally estimated. But it was not strong enough, and last-ditch measures to rush production of superb machines like the Me-262 jet fighters bogged down when needed parts and fuel failed to materialize. (*Left:* Me-262s abandoned by workers at jet assembly plant near Obertraubling Airdrome.) Those jets which reached air fighting hinted at Germany's regaining control of the air — but no more than hinted. They failed to retard the heavy bomber attacks which continued to turn the country into an industrial graveyard, like the Leuna synthetic oil works (*below*) at Merseburg. Months before Germany's armies capitulated, the nation had died from within.

Liberator high over Linz, Austria.

S/Sgt. Clarence E. Johnson, 8th Air Force.

Lt. Robert D. MacGeorge, 8th Air Force.

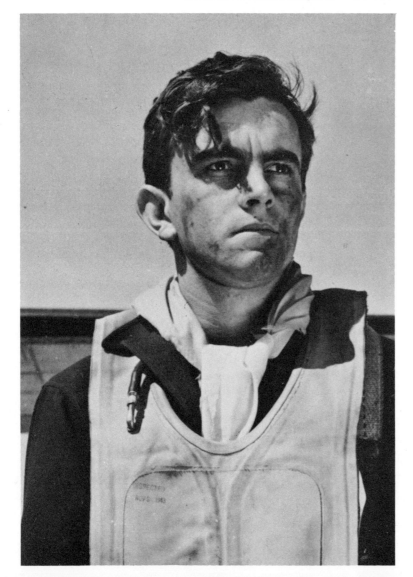

The strain and anxiety of long missions deep into Germany show clearly on the faces of the two men at the left. It was astonishing how the hours spent at high altitude could sap a man's strength, could bring him home to his base in England or Italy all washed out, eyes burning with fatigue and nerves taut. There were many reasons for this exhaustion — breathing for hours through an oxygen mask, below-zero cold, suffering from dehydration, feeling the jarring impact of enemy bullets and shells, watching your best friends in the next B-17 or B-24 trapped in their burning plane, unable to get out, wondering who was next.

Medal of Honor Citation: Technical Sergeant F.L. Vosler: ". . . a 20-mm cannon shell exploded in the radio compartment, painfully wounding Sgt. Vosler in the legs and thighs . . . with grim determination, [he] kept up a stream of deadly fire. Shortly thereafter another 20-mm enemy shell exploded, wounding Sgt. Vosler in the chest and about the face. Pieces of metal lodged in both eyes . . . he kept firing his guns . . ." There were more like Vosler. Many of them we know about. Others went down with their ships, their deeds lost for all time: gunners who refused to quit and kept firing until their bombers exploded on the ground — pilots who stayed in their burning planes because a man was wounded and couldn't bail out — bombardiers who remained glued to their sights when they were over target, determined to send several tons into a factory despite exploding cannon shells and bursting rockets and steel-jacketed bullets. There are statistics for tonnages dropped, for millions of rounds of ammunition expended, for sorties flown and for planes lost. . .but none for the ache of shattered bones and torn flesh, or of bodies seared by flaming gasoline. And there are none for the anguish of men who died on the ground — fliers all — like the eleven crew members who were almost entirely consumed when their Flying Fortress exploded and burned *(above)* waiting for the signal to take off.

The long final plunge

By spring of 1945 the German nation was whipped. Almost paralyzed industrially, its communications badly snarled, and its economy bled white, defeat — in the air as well as on the ground — was only a matter of time. The AAF statisticians had all manner of charts and graphs to prove this was so. Unfortunately, they could never represent with a squiggle on a graph the incredibly desperate last-ditch flying of the German fighter pilots. A B-17 shot down in flames three days before all was *kaput* carried down to the earth, miles below, eleven men who were just as dead as if they had "bought it" over Schweinfurt back in 1943. The sight of large groups of Me-262 jet fighters, and lesser numbers of the speedy Me-163 rocket

interceptor, still conjured up the nightmare that Hitler might yet produce a miracle in the struggle for air supremacy. On March 3, 1945, more than fifty of these new fighters playfully circled escorting P-51 Mustangs at tremendous speed, then closed in and shot down six heavy bombers and three fighters without loss. On March 18th — with our victory already assured — twenty-four bombers and five fighters out of 1,250 bombers and 850 fighters that attacked Berlin were shot down, sixteen other bombers were so badly damaged they crash-landed in Russian territory. And flak put some holes in nearly 700 bombers. The 550-mph speed of the Me-262 and the punch of its four 30-mm cannon proved devastating; one burst tore the wing clear off the hapless B-17 in the above picture. Despite the jets' superiority, they had come too late and were too few. We were right. Germany had her jets, but she lost the war.

The danger of flying close formations over Germany sometimes posed a threat greater than enemy fighter planes and flak. The Fortress cut in two *(above)* suffered no enemy blow. A formation lead ship, it was struck from behind and below by the propellers of a climbing plane which sliced it clean in two. No parachutes were seen as the B-17 plunged toward the earth five miles away.

Its fuselage, wings and tail ripped by enemy cannon shells, its wing fuel tanks, oxygen system and hydraulic lines aflame, this B-24 *(below)*, caught by enemy fighters over Austria, is heeled hard over in a steep bank. With the flames engulfing the entire airplane, it flipped wildly out of control, tumbled earthward. On the way down the tanks exploded, instantly killing the crew of ten.

It was during the campaign for the industrial Ruhr valley that the Luftwaffe played its most grisly trump card. Hermann Goering had begun his plans for a last violent try at our bombers more than a month before. In a special Order of the Day he called for pilots to volunteer for a secret, dangerous duty. Some 300 were selected and shipped to Stendal for a ten-day course in air ramming, most of which consisted of getting them into the right frame of mind by lectures, films and Nazi indoctrination. They were taught the technique of flying out of the sun on a line astern of the bombers, opening fire at extreme range, and holding it until the final sharp ramming dive just forward of the bomber's tail. They were allowed at the last minute to bail out, if possible (usually it wasn't). Eighty pilots were given FW-190s and sent to Prague to operate against the 15th Air Force; the remainder re-

ceived Me-109s and organized into units with the names of *Falken* and *Raubvogel* (birds of prey). On 7th, with 1,300 American heavy bombers and 850 fi in the air, the *Raubvogel* rose to do or die. In thei were dinned exhortations and patriotic music; the radio transmitters had been removed from their so that they could not talk back. AAF gunners *(a and pilots were startled at the wild combat man that ensued, but the Luftwaffe proved ineffective. the melee was over, 65 German planes had gone before our fighters; the bombers brought the to 104, and there is no estimate of how many Luf planes were destroyed by our 22 bombers and 3 fi which were lost. From April 5th to 19th, we almo nihilated what was left of the Luftwaffe — destr 3,484 planes in the air and on the ground.

Is the lesson learned?

The glowering, angry man in the photograph *(right)* has just been defeated. He finds this hard to believe after years of Nazi invincibility and conquest, and it will be many months before the true facts of life sink in — the vast German army whipped, her Navy destroyed, the Luftwaffe broken, and millions of German soldiers killed and wounded in air raids which inflicted hideous ruin on the Reich's cities, killing some half-million civilians and injuring seriously another million. Like many of his contemporaries, Lieutenant General Kurt Badinsky has a professional hatred for the heavy bombers *(above)* which spearheaded the destruction of the German nation. But this is unimportant. The big question — was the lesson learned?

Japanese hammered by day and night

AAF presses home attacks across Pacific, Asia

On August 14, 1945, the Japanese nation, still the military ruler of a billion people and a land area of some 3,000,000 square miles, admitted complete defeat. This admission, in the form of unconditional surrender, was forced on her as the result of a vast and well co-ordinated effort on the part of all arms of the United States — a triphibious assault in which airpower played the decisive part. A final assessment of the degree to which airpower contributed to Japan's defeat is complex and debatable. There was no one strategy employed against Japan, but rather a naval strategy and a land strategy which crumbled Japan's outer defenses and (with chief credit to our submarines) isolated the country from its overseas sources of raw materials. Yet, if we view the Pacific war objectively, the objective of combat operations in that far-flung theater was to advance airpower to the point where the full fury of crushing air attack could be

loosed on Japan itself, with the possibility that such attack would bring about the defeat of the enemy without invasion. This idea was scorned by naval and ground commanders as ridiculous, and they proceeded without hesitation toward a massive invasion which would likely have cost the United States 1,000,000 dead and wounded soldiers and marines. Yet, there was no invasion — despite the fact that the fanatical Japanase army had suffered little during the war, was still five million strong, and that the "near-panic caused within the U. S. Navy by Japan's suicide pilots" would be likely to be repeated when enemy fliers by the thousands threw themselves at our fleet. The Japanese capitulated because B-29s had virtually annihilated their urban centers, crushed the Japanese people's faith in the ability of their government to defend them, and turned industry into a wasteland of ash and rubble.

Mechanics fill the twin belly tanks of a P-38 fighter (*above*) in the Philippines with highly inflammable gasoline-impregnated jelly — napalm. Upon impact the bombs scattered sheets of furious flame; Japanese feared napalm more than all other weapons.

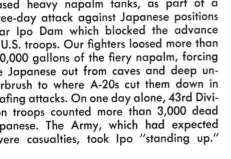

The P-38s in the above picture have just released heavy napalm tanks, as part of a three-day attack against Japanese positions near Ipo Dam which blocked the advance of U.S. troops. Our fighters loosed more than 200,000 gallons of the fiery napalm, forcing the Japanese out from caves and deep underbrush to where A-20s cut them down in strafing attacks. On one day alone, 43rd Division troops counted more than 3,000 dead Japanese. The Army, which had expected severe casualties, took Ipo "standing up."

While U.S. infantry and tank teams watched, P-38 fighters dove to within 75 yards of the American positions (*right*) to hurl heavy bombs in precision diving attacks into enemy fortifications in Batangas Province, Luzon Island. Fighters and infantry operated as close teams in the Philippines, the planes sometimes strafing and bombing only a few yards in front of our own men. Use of tactical airpower with ground forces killed tens of thousands of Japanese troops, prevented heavy American casualties.

A B-24 Liberator crew on their way home from a bombing mission in the Celebes was astonished to see a Japanese transport emerge suddenly from nearby clouds. B-24's top turret gunner opened fire, exploded the transport's left wing tank *(above)*. When tail covering burned off, the transport plunged into sea.

Hedge-hopping B-25 on the prowl for Japanese vehicles caught this truck *(above)* on a central Luzon highway, roared low in strafing and parafrag attack. Note soldier jumping for cover. Terrific blast of strings of parafrag bombs *(below)* tears apart trains, rails and buildings at Chickunan marshalling yards on Formosa.

The plight of desperate men is clearly evident in this photo *(above)* of stricken Japanese frigate (destroyer escort) which was caught and heavily bombed by B-25s of the Air Apaches Group near Amoy, China. Despite frantic maneuvering and defensive firing, the frigate received several direct hits with bombs which tore open her hull above and below the water line. As the sinking ship rolled over, her panic-stricken crew sprawled over her sides, clinging to lines and to wreckage in the sea. Rampaging bombers and fighters raised havoc with shipping along China coast, effectively stopped traffic to and from home islands.

The fine art of turning Japanese airfields into mass graveyards which had been perfected earlier in the war on New Guinea and New Ireland, reached its devastating climax in the Philippines, where hedge-hopping fighters and bombers wrecked more than one thousand enemy planes on the ground. Combined with massive carrier assaults, these attacks broke the back of enemy airpower in the islands, forced the Japanese to macabre *kamikaze* dives against our ships. At *right*, a string of parafrag bombs at the moment before they explode and destroy a bomber on Aparri Airdrome, Luzon. The reconnaissance plane at left was wrecked by the bomb blasts.

Ordnance men load 500-lb. bombs into a Convair B-24 Liberator *(above)* at a Palau airfield in the Caroline Islands. Heavy bomb load and effective combat range of 2,600 miles made Liberator Pacific heavyweight favorite. One of rarer AAF types in Pacific war was the Convair B-32 Dominator *(below)* shown on Okinawa field after a flight from Luzon. Dominators carried *forty* 500-lb bombs, had range of nearly 4,000 miles.

Dazed by almost unbelievable good fortune, Lt. S. F. Ford walks away unharmed from his wrecked and burning Lightning fighter *(above)*. Only seconds before Ford was caught at low speed and low altitude by Zero fighter which shot him down in flames. His P-38 hit the ground trailing fire, careened across open field, disintegrating as it ripped over plowed ground. Rugged construction of the big fighter saved his life. One P-38 at 300 mph hit telephone pole, bashed in wing, brought its pilot home.

Armorers load .50-caliber shells into nose guns of North American Mitchell *(right)* on Okinawa airfield. Assigned to 41st Bomb Group, B-25 had just completed strike over Kyushu, was going out again. Mitchells were turned into flying arsenals; fitted with eighteen heavy machine guns, they carried up to two tons of bombs, as well as rockets which were slung beneath the wings. They sank ships with fire power alone. Some versions had a 75-mm cannon plus fourteen guns.

Mitchell bombers carrying Mark 13 (GT-1) aerial torpedoes waiting on Okinawa airfield *(above)* to take off for a mission against shipping in a Kyushu harbor. First combat use of the new guided missiles was made on July 28, 1945, with B-25s of the 47th Bomb Squadron, 41st Bomb Group. Pilots disliked the winged torpedoes which restricted their bombing approach, felt that skip-bombing, preceded by heavy strafing, was the most effective means of sinking enemy ships. AAF first used missiles in 1943.

The greatest Tiger of them all — Major General Claire L. Chennault, who commanded the 14th Air Force in China, discusses maintenance problems with his mechanics. Applying the tactics he developed originally with the Flying Tigers, Chennault used his P-38, P-40, and P-51 fighters, B-24 and B-25 bombers in spectacular fashion against the Japanese. One of outstanding Far East maneuvers was the operation of a rampaging guerrilla force which flew from a network of six airfields located behind the enemy's lines. Chennault's fighters racked up a ten-to-one victory score over Japanese planes, and his fighters and bombers crippled enemy communications within China.

In an early morning mist, a Douglas C-47 transport *(above)* of the 1st Air Commando Group takes off from Tingkawks-Sagan airfield in Burma, destined for Allied forces in China. Transport operations in Burma and China were wild and hazardous; one major operation included the dropping of Ghurka troops and American engineers far behind Japanese lines to build guerrilla airfields, then supplying the isolated forces entirely by air drop and landings after treetop level flights in unarmed, helpless aircraft.

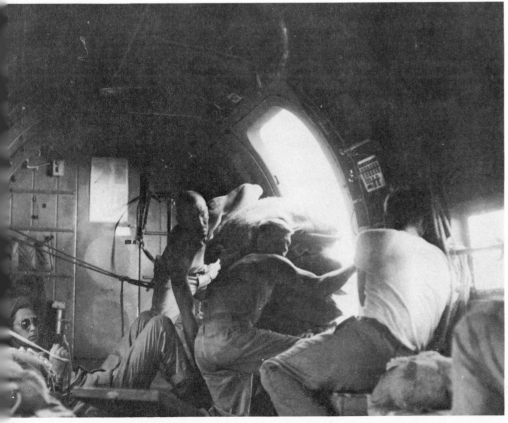

The three men in this C-47 transport poised to push heavy packages of supplies out the door of their airplane *(left)*, look toward the cockpit for the drop signal to be given by their pilot. With only small jungle clearings as their drop zones, the transport crews — this time on a mission to the Naga Hills, Upper Assam in India — had to time their drops perfectly with the pilot's signals. Helpless against air attack, these men faced death constantly—if they were shot down and captured, they would be brutally tortured.

Big, black and deadly, a Northrop P-61 Black Widow *(right)* flies out from its base on one of the Marianas Islands. Taking to the air between dusk and dawn, the twin-boomed, radar-equipped P-61s were the answer to Japanese planes which struck in night raids at the B-29 fields on Guam and Saipan from their base on Iwo Jima; Widows searched out the enemy with radar, destroyed them with eight guns and cannon.

Armorer-gunners of a 7th Air Force night-fighter squadron *(left)* in the Marianas load belted shells in the four heavy cannon carried by the Black Widow; airplane also has four .50-caliber guns in top turret. The P-61, the best night-fighter of the war, demoralized the enemy with its "uncanny" radar-directed attacks in darkness. They were loved by pilots who were lost over the sea at night, guided home by wistful Widows.

This North American P-51D Mustang being ferried on a Navy barge from a lighter to shore at Orote Bay, Guam, *(below)* provides an outstanding example of Pacific war co-operation. The islands wrested from Japan were transformed by vast engineering feats into great air-fields to move our bombers into position to strike enemy homeland.

Pilots of the VII Fighter Command who flew Mustangs from Iwo Jima *(right)* had some of the longest toughest missions ever undertaken by a fighter outfit. They flew in weather that earned every foul name in the Army's lexicon of abuse — on a June 1st mission, returning from Osaka, 24 P-51s caught in a seething cauldron of storms disappeared forever into the Pacific. Often the planes crashed on take-off, their engines fouled by Iwo Jima's gritty volcanic dust. On long escort or fighter sweep missions to Japan, jackknifed into the cockpits of their P-51s, pilots flew up to nine hours over 1,600 miles of sea, for only a few minutes' time in combat strafing or dueling enemy fighters. "A mission wasn't so bad after the first hour because your legs got numb," said one pilot, "but when you got home, you didn't feel much like sitting. You were raw."

This is a far cry from the "we live in fame, go down in flame" which characterized the air force to much of the public. The men lodged comfortably (if somewhat cramped) in this cave on Ie Shima island are part of the 318th Fighter Group, which flew P-47 sweeps against Japan, 650 miles to the north.

Republic P-47N Thunderbolt of crack 318th Fighter Group on Ie Shima. Powerful P-47Ns were the longest-ranging single-engine fighters in the world, flew missions of nine and one half hours from Ie Shima to Tokyo and return. Thunderbolt's tremendous speed and altitude, plus heavy firepower made it a fighter the Japanese feared, and on most occasions refused to fight.

THE PAY-OFF

B-29s burned Japan to the ground. In 69 cities, 178 square miles became funereal wastelands

By the end of July, 1945, some ninety large and small Japanese cities had become ash-filled deserts. Industry was strangled, with hundreds of millions of square feet of factory area destroyed. Hundreds of undamaged plants which had been ignored by the B-29s stood useless, denied the materials and the tools with which to work, and abandoned by their laborers who had fled to the hills in terror of future raids. A great torch had been applied to Japan, and the results could be appreciated only by seeing the mile after mile of blackened cinders, by smelling the horrifying mounds of the charred and bloated dead. It was a terrible punishment which, in five months of concentrated strategic air attack, had dealt Japan a mortal blow. In one night alone, B-29s sowed a great fire wind in Tokyo which generated temperatures exceeding 1,600 degrees F., engulfed and laid waste sixteen square miles, and burned to death an estimated 130,000 people — twice as many as died at Nagasaki. Many people in the Western world, hearing the B-29 crew descriptions of the enormous fires with statements such as "Tokyo caught fire like a forest of pine trees," were inclined to credit enthusiasm rather than facts as the source of these reports. But a Tokyo newspaperman sadly wrote that "Superfortress reports of damage . . . were not exaggerated; if anything, they constitute the most shocking understatement in the history of aerial warfare."

Toyama: 95.6% destroyed in one night; 10,000 people burned to death.

Vast engineering effort supported B-29 program

Each Superfortress airstrip on Saipan required a runway 200 feet in width and 8,500 feet long, six miles of taxiways and 180 parking hardstands. The engineering battalions *(left;* surveying an air-base site) which built the big airfields also established Kobler and Kagman Point airdromes for other bomber and fighter operations, carved out a network of roads, set up a 40,000 gallon tank farm, and in quick time had operating an asphalt plant and a coral pit with a capacity of 2,000 tons a day. To expedite moving the coral, Negro engineers of the 1894th Battalion in five days pounded out a hard-surface, three-mile highway, which reduced the truck haul from the coral pits to the airfield from five hours to fifteen minutes. General Curt LeMay condemned the Navy's grudging logistical support which put his air bases "91st on a list of priorities, below . . . fleet recreation [and] tennis courts." On islands to the north, the airfield construction and erection of supporting facilities went on for our fighters and bombers *(left;* setting up seawater pipeline for construction work on Ie Shima). The work of these men was every bit as vital as the pilots and gunners who manned the Superfortresses over Tokyo.

Asphalt plant on Guam Island (*above*) where more than 90,000 tons of crushed rock were mixed with 1,200,000 gallons of asphalt oil to top the runways and the three and one half miles of taxiways and hardstands in the construction of sprawling North Field.

Japanese attacked Marianas bases by day and night, bombing B-29s and other planes; explosions and fire consumed this Superfortress. Strong aerial defenses and heavy bombing of Iwo Jima all but stopped attacks; they ended when Marines invaded island.

Sheet metal workers of the 480th Service Squadron, 59th Service Group (above), repair flak damage on a B-29. Like the air war fought in Europe, the success or failure of combat missions depended upon skill of ground crews who kept planes in condition.

A B-29 armorer at Guam (left) concentrates on his precise job of inserting a fuze into the tail of a 500-lb. demolition bomb. The enormous size of the B-29's twin bomb bays can be appreciated in this photograph; the demolition bombs were destined for a steel-and-concrete aircraft factory on Honshu. B-29s carried up to ten tons of bombs per plane against Japan, as compared to the two tons averaged by Flying Fortresses.

Complex and backbreaking task of attending to B-29 maintenance is evident in this shot of ground crewmen (right) changing one of the huge wheels on one landing-gear leg. Grossing more than 60 tons loaded, the enormous airplane was filled with complex electronic equipment which demanded perfect servicing. Its remote-control armament, pressurized compartment, new radar and navigational aids, twin bomb bays, new design double-tire undercarriage — all these and other features compounded the responsibilities of the ground crews.

Sowing the fire winds

The most difficult incendiary target in all Japan was Nagoya — known to B-29 crews as "the city that wouldn't burn." Bombing accuracy was poor, and despite repeated heavy attacks, areas razed were free of industry, and fire sweep was limited. On the night of May 17th, the B-29s returned for a knockout blow, dumped 3,609 tons of incendiaries which wiped out 3.87 square miles of south Nagoya. In the midst of the wreckage lay the gutted Mitsubishi aircraft assembly plants, largest in Japan. After taking four mass incendiary and nine other attacks, and costing the AAF fifty-eight B-29s, Nagoya *(left)* was finally crossed off the target list. Most satisfying target was Mitsubishi No. 4; producer of 40 per cent of all Japan's engines, it was 96 per cent destroyed by demolition and incendiary bombs. The destruction of Nagoya was particularly disastrous for the Japanese. The Mitsubishi aircraft manufacturing complex was one of the world's largest, and in parts of the city factories stretched for miles. We also had help in Nagoya; early in December of 1944 severe earthquakes ripped through the city and stopped all production for several days.

The Musashino aircraft-engine plant in Tokyo, which manufactured up to 2,800 radial engines per month, became the most bombed and the most missed of all enemy targets. Finally it was left in a state of ruin. One half of the plant, built of reinforced concrete, was relatively undamaged, but its machines ground to a halt when precision strikes with bombs up to two tons in weight destroyed the other half of the factory *(right)*. In a twin attack in May, two days apart, 984 B-29s hurled 7,000 tons of incendiaries into Tokyo, wiped out 22 square miles of shadow factories in homes, the Ginza commercial area, the government and embassy districts, and the zone surrounding the imperial palace. In seven major raids, B-29s dropped 11,836 tons of bombs, destroyed 56.3 square miles (the industrial half) of Tokyo's total area of 111 square miles. It was crossed off the target list.

One fact became certain in the wealth of data concerning the heavy B-29 attacks against Japan — the Superfortress was a superb combat weapon which had withstood the full force of Japanese fighters, 969 of which were shot down. It could absorb great punishment, and it was deadly to enemy planes. In January, 1945, when Japanese fighter attacks were pressed home with wild-flying pilots, B-29 losses rose to their highest of the war — 5.7% of all attacking planes. Combat reports tell how "fanatical hopped-up pilots pressed their attacks right down the formations' stream of fire, dove into formations to attempt rammings *(above: a twin-engined Nick barely misses a B-29's wing)*, and sprayed fire at random." But by June, 1945, with night incendiary raids the major method of attack, losses dropped to less than one percent.

Statement from Jiro Horikoshi, Japan's outstanding aeronautical engineer: "Many a factory which went through the time-consuming steps of dispersing its most important machine and assembly lines now found itself no better off than before dispersal. The B-29s relentlessly and literally tracked down every move. . . . The plant managers searched frantically for new sites, and sought refuge in factory buildings surrounded by steep mountains, or placed their vital machines within emergency caves drilled into the sides of hills. Eventually the dispersal plan proved to be a complete failure. At the time when we most desperately needed production, our industrial personnel scrabbled in the hills. . . . Devastation in Japan mounted daily." There was no way out for Japan. With factories gutted, dispersal a failure, the future held total ruin.

Majestic skies and death by fire

The statistics for personnel attrition in the B-29 campaign to burn Japan out of the war show that, despite the approximately 3,000 men who went down over the enemy's homeland, only 1 per cent of the crews on bombing missions were lost. There are even statistics which prove that "we were able to reduce Japan more economically than Germany." This matter of economy is carried to the point where we know that it cost only one B-29 and eleven dead men to wipe out each 3.5 square miles of cities with populations of less than 100,000. But no matter how it totals up, 414 B-29s shot down by fighters and flak meant a great many good men who never came home. Like the air war over Germany, death over Japan could be a matter of a split second when a plane blew up in a clean, brilliant flash — or it might be slow. This B-29 (above) is about to go down in a setting of cathedral-like majesty over Kobe.

The B-29 was a big and powerful airplane, and it took a lot to kill a 60-ton bomber. The fighters had a hard time of it, but no plane that ever flew can survive a direct hit with heavy flak — like the B-29 *(above)* hurtling down with its left wing blown completely off.

Japanese antiaircraft at times could be devastatingly accurate — the B-29 *(right)* tumbling crazily toward the city of Nagoya had its wing blown off by a direct hit, which also exploded the fuel tanks (the flaming mass at top center is a wing fuel cell). A hit like this almost always condemned a crew; the centrifugal force created by the bomber's spinning and tumbling often trapped each crewman within the airplane— and kept him there until the fatal impact.

One engine damaged by flak and feathered, a crippled Boeing B-29 Superfortress eases down to a dirt runway on Iwo Jima in an emergency landing. In six months, 2, 251 Superfortresses landed on the tiny island. Rescue operations on Iwo Jima started with a crude dirt runway that barely accommodated the first B-29 — which was refueled by gasoline carried in helmets of Marines.

Haven at Iwo

To every B-29 crewman who flew to Japan after March, 1945, the fact that Iwo Jima had become a United States base was a cause for thanksgiving. Iwo is eight miles long — a little island. But never did so little mean so much to so many. Located about midway between Guam and Japan, Iwo broke the long stretch, coming and going. If a B-29 had engine trouble, it held out for Iwo. If the plane was shot up over Japan and had wounded aboard, the pilot went for Iwo. If the weather was too rough and gas was low, the bombers headed for Iwo. Formations assembled over the volcanic rock, and gassed up at Iwo Jima for extra-long missions. Fighter escort usually came from its dusty airstrips. And if crews had to ditch or bail out over the sea, they knew that air-sea rescue units would come from Iwo Jima. From March 4th, when the first crippled Superfortress touched its wheels down, to the end of the war, 2,251 of the great B-29s landed at Iwo. A large number of these would have been lost if the little island had not been in American hands — and each of the B-29s carried eleven men, for a total of 24,761 fliers who brought their crippled bombers down to safety, 650 miles from nowhere. It cost the United States Marines the terrible price of more than 5,000 dead and 16,000 wounded to take Iwo from the Japanese — an accomplishment for which every man who served with the 20th Air Force and the VII Fighter Command is eternally grateful. No one more regretted those casualties than General Henry H. Arnold. On July 14, 1944, one month after the invasion of Saipan, Arnold recommended seizure of Iwo Jima. It was October before the Joint Chiefs acted on Arnold's proposal; the invasion finally was set for January, then postponed to its actual date of February 19, 1945. But what the military heads never knew was that seven months before, when Arnold recommended invasion, the Japanese had written Iwo Jima off as lost, *and abandoned the island.* Only after United States' attention was diverted elsewhere did they return to turn Iwo into the fortress which killed or wounded 21,000 U. S. Marines.

With one engine shot out and the propeller feathered, a crippled B-29 heads for Iwo Jima. Picture was taken from "buddy" Superfortress which reduced its speed and escorted other plane home, to foil attacks by Japanese fighters. AAF moved complete servicing and maintenance facilities into Iwo Jima for B-29s, as well as for fighters which made escort missions against Japan.

Tight-lipped B-29 commander sweats out low fuel supply on return to Saipan *(right)* while his flight engineer looks on. Headwinds over Japan reached velocities greater than 200 mph — pilots occasionally reported that these winds held their B-29s motionless in the air, or pushed them back to sea! On ocean below bombers' homeward flight, U.S. Navy maintained elaborate rescue organization which saved hundreds of men.

With or without atom bomb, B-29s had burned Japan out of the war

The atomic bombs dropped by men of the 509th Composite Group (at a target-class study; *above*) stunned the world and ushered in a new era of war, but they arrived at a time when Japan was already beaten. The devastation at Hiroshima *(below)* and Nagasaki was ap-

palling, but it added only 3 per cent to the area already burned out of Japan's target cities. Hiroshima suffered 80,000 dead and 4.6 square miles destroyed; in one night B-29s killed 130,000 people, and burned to the ground 16 square miles of Tokyo.

The smoke from the explosion of the first atomic bomb billowing 20,000 feet over Hiroshima; the towering mushroom cloud reached a height of more than eight miles (twelve miles at Nagasaki). Two B-29s of the 509th Composite Group, part of the 313th Wing of the 20th Air Force, participated in the first atomic bombing mission in history, on August 5, 1945. One of the Superfortresses carried the bomb, the other flew as escort, carrying special instruments and cameras to record explosion data.

The future promised only ruin

For the two young Japanese pilots in this picture, the world has just come to an end. Led to believe all their lives in the righteousness and the invincibility of their country, convinced after lifelong indoctrination that no Japanese ever surrenders, that in submission there is only disgrace — they have just flown the Japanese surrender mission from their homeland to the bleak island of Ie Shima. For even the Japanese, with all their myopic shortcomings, could read the handwriting on the wall. The future of Japan held only ruin piled upon ruin, it promised a devastating assault from the air which would pale

to insignificance all that which had already struck the Japanese islands. It was a difficult move for the Japanese to make, to overthrow in a single move the beliefs of centuries, to admit that death in a futile battle was not the proper destiny for the eighty million people of Japan. But because American airpower threatened virtually to turn Japan into ashes, the Japanese surrendered. Their nation's capitulation, forced by the two atomic attacks, came as a surprise to most Japanese, who until the final day of war heard only that the bombings would hearten all Japanese to redoubled efforts to carry on to final victory. It is bitter irony that the radio station which spewed forth this fatalistic nonsense, and which exhorted them to do or die despite the B-29s, was Station JOAK.

Why there was no invasion of Japan

NO SHORTAGE OF RESPONSIBILITY

New developments in air technology confirmed worst fears of AAF strategists: America now lay exposed to devastating polar attack

The day that World War II ended, the military maps which hung on the walls of Air Force operations rooms became obsolete. The potentials of aircraft performance promised by the jet engine, by guided missiles projects, and by intercontinental range bombers — all of which were in existence while the shooting in the Pacific was still going on — meant that the geographical packets into which military maps were broken down had become meaningless colored blots. There are no arbitrary geographical restrictions known to the intercontinental bomber. The new air age which was ushered in by the extraordinary technological developments of the war underscored the fact that the shortest route between an enemy nation and the United States no longer was determined by bases around the world . . . rather, it was a curved line across the top of the globe. In another war,

this polar region would become no man's land. It did not take expert knowledge to realize soon after hostilities had ceased that the Soviet Union was engaged in a maximum effort to construct a great intercontinental air fleet, properly armed with nuclear weapons, and that if the United States itself were not able to strike anywhere in Russia, immediately and with overwhelming force, the days of this country were numbered.

The nightmare finally was realized — the air routes across the polar regions were open. A devastating attack with little or no warning had progressed from theory into imminent possibility. This was the thinking in the early postwar years which shaped Air Force planning and led to the creation on March 21, 1946, of the Strategic Air Command; it also spurred the fight for an autonomous USAF which finally was gained in 1947.

Why there was no invasion of Japan

NO SHORTAGE OF RESPONSIBILITY

New developments in air technology confirmed worst fears of AAF strategists: America now lay exposed to devastating polar attack

The day that World War II ended, the military maps which hung on the walls of Air Force operations rooms became obsolete. The potentials of aircraft performance promised by the jet engine, by guided missiles projects, and by intercontinental range bombers — all of which were in existence while the shooting in the Pacific was still going on — meant that the geographical packets into which military maps were broken down had become meaningless colored blots. There are no arbitrary geographical restrictions known to the intercontinental bomber. The new air age which was ushered in by the extraordinary technological developments of the war underscored the fact that the shortest route between an enemy nation and the United States no longer was determined by bases around the world . . . rather, it was a curved line across the top of the globe. In another war,

this polar region would become no man's land. It did not take expert knowledge to realize soon after hostilities had ceased that the Soviet Union was engaged in a maximum effort to construct a great intercontinental air fleet, properly armed with nuclear weapons, and that if the United States itself were not able to strike anywhere in Russia, immediately and with overwhelming force, the days of this country were numbered.

The nightmare finally was realized — the air routes across the polar regions were open. A devastating attack with little or no warning had progressed from theory into imminent possibility. This was the thinking in the early postwar years which shaped Air Force planning and led to the creation on March 21, 1946, of the Strategic Air Command; it also spurred the fight for an autonomous USAF which finally was gained in 1947.

Far out over the Arctic Ocean, a Boeing B-29 Superfortress of the 375th Reconnaissance Squadron wings its way toward the North Pole on a combat-reconnaissance and weather-information mission. As the mainstay of the USAF in the early postwar years, the B-29 was modified continually to take new electronic and combat equipment. Carrying atomic weapons, the postwar B-29 fleet gave the United States airpower of unprecedented dimension, and for years it remained the greatest single striking weapon in existence. Carrying an atomic bomb, and operating from air bases on the North American continent, the airplane could strike in one-way missions against the Soviet Union; with air refueling, it gained the range necessary to carry its crews beyond Russian territory. Admittedly an obsolescent and an interim weapon, it held the line while newer bombers were being built.

A new breed in the air

The superbly designed airplane at left is America's first combat jet fighter — the Lockheed P-80 Shooting Star. A product of World War II, it was designed, built and test-flown while its predecessors were destroying the German and the Japanese air forces. The day that the Shooting Star first took wing, every other airplane then flying with the AAF became obsolescent. For the Shooting Star was more than a new fighter plane — it was the first of an entire new breed which in one fell swoop advanced fighter speeds by more than a hundred miles per hour, and hurled pilots and planes into the maw of severe compressibility — the "sound barrier" — and the host of problems which attend flight at very high speeds. Pilots who first saw the beautiful lines of the new jet airplane feared for its structural strength; they did not see how the gracefully sweeping curves of the Shooting Star and its contemporaries could embody the solidity and ruggedness of World War II fighters. But jets are designed to withstand the tremendous forces of transonic flight, and as such they are fighter planes with great structural strength. With their new-found power and performance, the jet fighters heralded the end of all existing bombers — the deadly success of the Messerschmitt Me-262 against the B-17s and B-24s, ignored by many who cried out against the postwar expenditure of staggering sums for the research and development of new jet bombers, was to be repeated in Korea when swift MiG-15s tore through F-86 escorts to attack B-29s and demonstrated in unarguable terms that a new war cannot be fought with the weapons of the old.

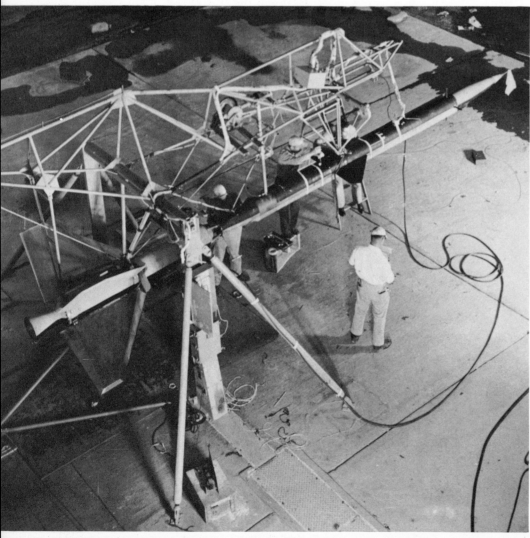

The advent of jet fighters called for more than new production techniques and improved flight procedures — it meant an entire new force of jet mechanics, with all their required equipment and tools, had to be developed. The USAF's vast ground force, like the ground crew in the above picture, proved itself more than equal to the task. While fire bursts from the tail cone of a Thunderjet fighter of the 33rd Fighter Group, mechanics carefully check operation of fuel lines and other parts. Later they reassembled the 600-mph fighter. The 33rd F.G. in 1948 flew interception missions from Cape Cod.

That it would require an entire new weapons system to combat jet bombers of the future was recognized by the Air Force as far back as the final months of World War II. In 1945 the Boeing Airplane Company instituted work for the AAF on a new line of anti-bomber missiles, known as GAPA (above), which attained speeds in test flights greater than 1,500 mph. In a program which extended for four years, the Boeing company fired more than 100 of the sleek weapons in different versions, testing electronic homing devices, power plants, instruments, launching equipment, and other material. Thus the GAPA became the direct forerunner of today's ground-to-air missiles.

Designed to specifications laid down in 1941, and under construction during the war, the massive Convair B-36 became the USAF's first-line strategic bomber several years after World War II. The largest bomber ever built (it is still unsurpassed in size), the six-engined B-36 gave the USAF an airplane which could reach from continental bases to any target in the world. For the first time in our history, we had in existence the weapon needed to maintain peace in a time of potential war — with nuclear bombs, the B-36 kept the USSR at bay for years. At right, a B-36 undergoing tests at Ladd AFB.

One of the most advanced aerodynamic machines ever to fly in this country was Northrop's XB-35 Flying Wing, a 105-ton bomber designed to achieve maximum efficiency through a radical all-wing design. Like the B-36, the XB-35 design was begun before W. W. II and, again like the Convair product, it first flew in 1946. Featuring high speed and a range of 7,000 miles, the XB-35 held the greatest promise of any USAF airplane. The problems encountered in its development delayed the program, however, and despite fifteen airplanes built, which include the eight-jet YB-49, the Northrop program yielded to a B-36 production order; the latter ranged 10,000 miles and had a bomb capacity which reached 42 tons.

The unexpected boomerang...

The Berlin Airlift

Hunger is a weapon that can kill a city as effectively as fire bombs or the steel fist blast of an atomic explosion. In June, 1948, making one of their first open moves against their former Allies, the Russians called upon hunger as their ally in the battle for the city of Berlin. Except for three air corridors, each twenty miles in width, the Soviets sealed off 2,500,000 people of Germany's capital from the outside world. On minimum rations, two and a quarter million people require at least 4,500 tons of food and fuel daily. The task of supplying the needed goods seemed unsurmountable. The USAF gambled that the impossible could be done and called on General Curtis LeMay, the man who had burned Japan out of the war, to do the job. Two- and four-engine transports were requisitioned from around the world. They collected on Rhein-Main and other airfields in the Allied occupation zones, and then they began Operations Vittles to keep Berlin alive and free. It was a success beyond all expectation; airpower had beaten the Russians in the first battle of the Cold War. On September 18th, in weather so foul that instrument flying was mandatory 18 of the 24 hours, the aerial task force hauled 5,583 tons into Berlin in 652 flights — a remarkable feat of disciplined flying. The USAF total for the airlift was 1,783,826 tons.

GCA radar operators performed wonders *(left)* in bringing transports safely into Templehof through blinding fog, haze *(right)*.

The tremendous advances in long-range bomber performance, coupled with the threat of nuclear attacks upon American cities at night or in storms, prompted the need for swift-climbing and heavily armed jet interceptors which could seek out enemy raiders under any and all flying conditions. The first of these radar-directed fighters was Lockheed's F-94 Starfire (above; during high-altitude patrol); latest versions still defend U.S.

A postwar development of the B-29 was the Boeing B-50 Super-fortress which, although resembling its predecessor, was a 75% new design. Its four new 3,500-hp engines boosted power by 59%, increased the airplane's speed to 400 mph, and enabled it to carry five tons of bombs 6,000 miles without refueling. With new air-refueling techniques such as the Flying Boom allowed, the B-50 gained intercontinental range with atomic weapons.

In 1950 the USAF launched this Bumper rocket *(below)*, consisting of a captured V-2 as the first stage, and a WAC corporal as the boosted missile. The tests from Cape Canaveral in Florida demonstrated for the first time practical separation techniques in horizontal flight of large step-rockets, a major break-through in development of long-range missiles. Since its opening, Canaveral has been the launching center for USAF's 5,000-mile test range.

Another wartime-developed airplane which USAF used to break down serious aerodynamic problems impeding development of supersonic combat aircraft was the spectacular, stubby, rocket-powered X-1. First flown with rocket power on December 10, 1946, the X-1 ten months later ripped past sonic speed, went on to achieve its record-breaking maximum of 963 mph before being retired with honors to the Smithsonian Institution. The X-1 was a brilliant example of superior American aeronautical engineering, both by the USAF and the Bell company. As the first airplane to exceed supersonic speeds in level flight, it exploded the myth of the lethal "sound barrier," disproved the arguments of German engineers that only sweptwing planes could fly past the speed of sound. With its Bell-produced successor models, the X-1 paved the way for new USAF fighters, now in production, which have achieved Mach 2.9 speeds.

Longer legs for bombers and a thrust into space

Its rocket booster streaming brilliant flame, a B-61 Matador missile hurtles into the air at Cape Canaveral in Florida, headed down the Missile Test Range over the Carribean. First USAF operational missile, the B-61 (new designation: TM-61) was withheld from field service until guidance equipment guaranteed high accuracy.

KOREA: AT THE EDGE OF WW III

Sabre pilot Captain L. M. Moore describes kill against MiG-15 fighters. MiG-15 was faster, could outmaneuver and fly at higher altitudes than heavier, long-ranging Sabres.

The United States Air Force in Korea had two specific missions after the initial enemy assault: to destroy the enemy's air force, and to deny the enemy the capability to launch and to sustain a general offensive. Both of these goals were met brilliantly. The Communists in Korea committed the fatal error of underestimating our airpower, its mobility and flexibility, and its effectiveness against their advancing army. In the initial fighting the Air Force by volume of firepower delivered over the whole of the enemy's forces weakened and then pinned down the North Korean Army's advance until the UN forces could be consolidated on the Pusan perimeter. Then, by an interdiction program so comprehensive and sustained that it amounted to vertical envelopment of the enemy's ground forces the USAF opened the way for the breakout from Pusan and spearheaded the annihilation of the North Korean Army. The intervention by Chinese forces was a serious planning error on our part; it caught us by surprise. Once this surprise effect of the mass assault from the Yalu was spent, however, crushing attrition from the air disrupted the Chinese supply lines and destroyed their rear areas to the point where the ground front finally became stabilized. The Communist armies were battered continually until they could move no farther. And at this point, with our air strength steadily bleeding the enemy on the ground, the UN forces occupying territory in North Korea merely maintained their front-line positions.

General James A. van Fleet: "The war that does the most damage to the enemy is from the air. It is an almost one-service war that goes on, air war, doing the damage

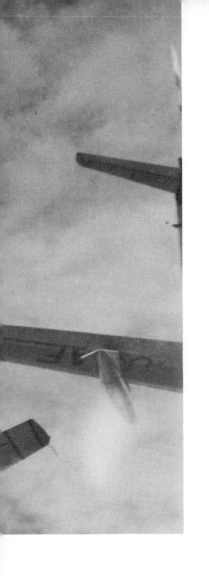

The **Korean War** added further laurels to the record of the B-29 *(right)*. One B-29 set a new record by flying 73,200 miles in one month. B-29s flew 1,076 days of the 1,106-day air war, dropped 160,000 tons of bombs —a greater tonnage than was needed to burn Japan out of World War II. After destroying Korea's industrial targets, B-29s flew tactical missions to support army.

to the enemy deep in his own territory." The Air Force was given a specific mission: stop the enemy on the ground, prevent him from breaking out. The USAF followed its order to the letter. During the two years of negotiations preceding the signing of the truce, the USAF with careful design immobolized and hammered the enemy until he was brought to an armistice on acceptable terms. Airpower was a bludgeon wielded freely across the conference table; when the Chinese became overly obstinate, battlefield pressure from the air was applied to achieve the desired diplomatic-military results.

The jet air war fought high over Korea will go down in history as even more significant than the Battle of Britain. The MiG-15 was the best product of Soviet air science. If this peak of Russian airpower had proven able to whip our F-86 *(above)* then the Russians were assured of air supremacy over Asia. There would have been no force capable of stemming a massive Russian push into their main target of Japan, then throughout the Far East. For with air supremacy in their hands — what was to stop the Russians? A badly outnumbered Army, or a Navy naked to overwhelming Russian air assault? No one has put this truism forth so clearly as General Curtis E. LeMay: "Once you have won the airpower battle, then there is no doubt about the outcome — the ultimate decision. You may or may not have to go in and destroy other military forces in being and in resources, but the survival of one nation's airpower over that of another decides the issue."

Two squadrons of F-86 Sabre fighters won the opening round of what might have been World War III in the thin, cold air high over Korea. They won that battle with a startling 14-to-one victory ratio, despite their being outnumbered, and forced to fight against an enemy air force whose bases were protected by diplomatic immunity. Had not these few planes, and their pilots, achieved mastery of the air, there is a probability that Russian air victory in Korea would eventually have been followed by the explosions of atomic and hydrogen bombs over American cities.

The setting sun silhouettes a Douglas B-26 (formerly A-26) Invader *(above)* of the 3rd Bomb Wing, being readied for an intruder mission. A World War II veteran, Invader was world's best attack bomber in Korean War. They struck enemy vehicles, troops, airfields, rail lines in hours of darkness, when Reds tried to reinforce their troops without interference from day raids. Invaders carried eighteen guns, two tons of bombs and rockets.

Armorers work through the night *(below)* readying guns of a North American F-86 Sabre for dawn patrol over North Korea. Sabre pilots were put at combat disadvantage by MiG-15s which flew several thousand feet higher, were faster and more maneuverable. But heavier F-86's firepower, rugged construction, electronic equipment and superior USAF piloting eliminated MiG's advantages, gave our fliers brilliant 14 to 1 kill superiority.

Carrying more than a ton of high-explosive bombs, rockets and ammunition, a Republic F-84 Thunderjet *(above)* of the 49th Fighter Bomber Wing thunders off a Korean airfield with an assist from auxiliary rocket boosters. Thunderjets and Shooting Stars did a tremendous ground-support job in Korea, many times averted disaster for ground forces which faced overwhelming numbers of the enemy. Ability of these jet fighter-bombers to absorb severe damage from enemy ground fire (considered worse than any encountered in World War II) and continue to fly, astonished their pilots. Obsolescent F-80s and F-84s flew their ground missions while the faster Sabres engaged Russian fighters.

Framed in the water pattern created by its whirling blades, a USAF air-rescue Sikorsky H-19 helicopter swoops low over the Han River near Seoul to pick up a downed pilot. During Korean fighting helicopters proved their worth by making nearly 1,000 actual rescues at sea and on land, behind enemy lines. The choppers flew thousands of missions evacuating wounded from isolated areas along the front lines, carried supplies to garrisons on islands off the Korean coast. U.S. Marines used the big Sikorsky helicopters to airlift rocket barrage teams behind enemy lines; troops fired heavy streams of rockets, then were picked up by helicopters to new positions, confusing enemy artillery.

A T-6 Mosquito spotter plane of the Fifth Air Force's 6147th Tactical Control Group in a steep bank as its crew searches for enemy forces on the ground. Flying the slow, unarmed, W.W. II North American training planes, Mosquito pilots proved indispensable during Korean fighting, were manned by courageous pilots who flew their fragile planes through the worst of enemy ground fire. After spotting enemy positions, the T-6 marked the area with a smoke rocket or a white phosphorus grenade, then called in fighter-bombers to take care of the situation with machine guns, rockets, cannon, bombs and napalm. Mosquito planes gave ground forces the closest possible air support.

Members of a Tactical Air Control Group *(right)* use their high-frequency radio to call in fighter-bombers to hit enemy positions on the Korean front. The jeep-equipped teams roamed the territory along and behind the front lines, working closely with the infantry to provide fighter-bomber support when required. Napalm bombs *(below)* dropped by B-26 Invaders of the 452nd Light Bomb Wing explode in fiery mushrooms against railroad cars in a marshalling yard along the main rail line leading south from Wonsan, a vital east-coast port city. Communist rail network especially took a beating in Korea; Reds finally moved trains only at night to escape day attacks, were then hit by intruders.

A classic example of the effects of infantry support is given by this Douglas B-26 Invader *(above)* which has just hurled a napalm tank with unerring accuracy against a Communist observation point in Korea. The hill was held by fanatic Chinese troops; well dug in, they were unaffected by heavy shellfire, rockets and other weapons, and constantly repulsed with heavy losses our troops. The searing napalm burst into the deep caves, and then burned the Chinese alive; our forces took the hill with ease.

This dramatic photo of a Lockheed F-80 fighter-bomber *(right)* captures the action which occurred when day-long flights of Fifth Air Force planes blasted the Communist supply center at Suan in one of the largest air strikes of the war. The supply area was smothered by more than 12,000 gallons of napalm — one napalm tank can be seen falling just below the airplane's left wing. General James A. van Fleet, deploring the inability of his own army to capitalize on the effects of these air attacks, stated: "If the army had been adequately supplied with ammunition, and could put a fire pressure on the enemy greater than it does now, it would consume more of the enemy, the enemy supplies, create problems for him which, in turn, would help our air service."

Small wars and forgotten heroes

In October, 1950, the UN forces, having suffered a succession of severe defeats at the hands of the North Koreans, sprung a surprise in the fighting with the first use of airborne troops. At Kimpo airfield, near Seoul, eighty twin-boomed Fairchild C-119 Packets of the 314th Troop Carrier Group and forty Douglas C-47s of the 21st Troop Carrier Squadron loaded 4,100 paratroopers of the Army's 187th Regimental Combat Team. The C-47 was an old veteran of prewar commercial flying and combat missions around the globe during World War II; the C-119 (above), a newcomer to battle with the USAF, was designed originally for the invasion of Japan. At altitudes of about 700 feet, the men of the 187th jumped near the villages of Sunchon and Sukchon, behind enemy lines and north of the North Korean capital. Fighting against surprised enemy units, they took the villages and set up roadblocks on the two principal highways which the Communists retreating from Pyongyang would have to use. For two days the men of the 187th fought with their airborne supplies alone; it was the first time paratroopers as they jumped had taken with them major equipment, including 105-mm howitzers, heavy machine guns and mortars, jeeps and trucks. Five months later 3,300 men made the war's second jump, dropping in a zone about 21 miles north of Seoul, and later successfully joined with armor driving northward. The paratroopers (left) and the men who flew the transports had come a long way since the first mass drops in Europe.

AIRPOWER TODAY

In the jet engine, nuclear weapons and avionics the scientist has placed in the hands of the air strategist the tools which have allowed him to produce drastic changes not only in the techniques of strategic air bombardment, but in the art of war itself. The awesome power of the nuclear and thermonuclear weapons makes it possible quickly to destroy a nation's means to exist, let alone to wage war. Since 1945 the foundation stone of United States national defense has been our power to wage strategic air war. When during the last decade budgets and manpower were cut, the USAF sacrificed its air defense and tactical strength so that the Strategic Air Command could be built up to the point where it could deliver, anywhere and at any time, the explosive power to eliminate any nation or bloc of nations. From the beginning our strategic air policy has been shaped by atomic realism; never again in war will there be time to fill out professional cadres with green men or to mobilize our industrial resources. The heart of American airpower today is the Strategic Air Command, and there is no reserve fat in SAC. It is a first-line striking force, constantly in a state of readiness, the strongest possible deterent to war. This is the thinking which molds the rest of the United States Air Force — we must be ready at all times to fight with the weapons on hand. It is a simple problem. If we are not ready . . . the nation will die.

The **92-ton bomber** plunging at the camera *(left)* is the current mainstay of the Strategic Air Command — the six-engine Boeing B-47 Stratojet, of which some 2,000 have been built. Spotted at air bases around the world the B-47, a medium, not a heavy long-range bomber, gains intercontinental striking power through air-to-air refueling. The three-man crew of the B-47 consists of a pilot, co-pilot, and a "three-headed monster," one man who serves the triple role of navigator, bombardier and radar operator. Since December, 1947, installation of new avionic devices and the use of missiles keeps the Stratojet a first-line strategic weapon.

A Martin B-57 of the Tactical Air Command streaks low over simulated enemy targets as its bomb explodes directly behind the airplane *(right)*. Replacing the B-26 Invader as the USAF's first-line night intruder, the B-57 (developed from the RAF's Canberra) gives TAC an all-weather light jet bomber for both day and night operations. Fast, highly maneuverable, and capable of operating at extreme heights, the B-57 performs the role of a light and a fighter-bomber in one. Its design characteristics allow for multiplicity of combat duties, together with the Douglas B-66 now entering operational service, it brings to the USAF an all-jet tactical bomber force for combat operations. Both the B-57 and B-66 are the last subsonic light bombers; new machines will be supersonic.

A flight of North American F-86 Sabres of the 21st Fighter Wing moves out shortly after sunrise at Goose Bay, Labrador, for a transocean flight to a USAF base at Narsarssuak, Greenland. Formerly assigned to George Air Force Base in California, the 21st Fighter Wing transferred in 1954 to a new air base at Chambley in northeastern France, to become part of the U.S. contribution to NATO. Later models of the F-86 which fought in Korea, the new Sabres maintained for the USAF a fighter force equal to the best of the USSR, its only potential air enemy. Latest versions of the Sabre fighter are modified to keep the airplane a first-line combat machine. The powerful F-86 also serves as the first-line fighter for the Royal Air Force, for Canada and for Australia, for Japan, and in an all-weather version for Italy. Its USAF replacement is the supersonic F-100.

The USAF's longest-ranging operational fighter plane, a Republic F-84F Thunderstreak, eases up beneath the suspended flying boom of a Boeing KB-29 tanker plane to refuel. Capable of speeds exceeding 700 mph, the rugged Thunderstreak performs a wide range of missions for USAF, extending from fighter-bomber and day fighter to a strategic reconnaissance plane and a strategic atomic bomber, when operating with the giant GRB-36G airplane. On test flights, carried in the belly of the ten-engined bomber, F-84Fs (as well as the RF-84F Thunderflash version) have carried out simulated combat missions exceeding 10,000 miles in range. Airplane's high speed, great load-carrying capacity, and armament make it a powerful addition to the USAF's fighter stable.

Every jet flier sits atop a giant firecracker. Beneath his seat is an explosive charge which in an emergency, after jettisoning his canopy, he uses to blow himself and his seat far above his speeding plane. Ejection at the high speeds of jet fighters can be a terrifying and a brutal experience; wind blast can snatch the helmet and oxygen mask of a pilot from his face in a hundredth of a second. Upon ejection, seats may tumble or spin violently, creating critical G forces, and snapping arms and legs. One of the main research programs of the Wright Air Development Center is to produce ejection equipment which protects the pilot, allows him safely to abandon a stricken aircraft. In this picture a WADC Aircraft Laboratory test ejects a dummy and seat from a fast-rolling F-94C fighter on the ground to demonstrate upward ejection capabilities. In a few seconds the dummy separated from the seat, reached a peak height of 45 feet, and was lowered to the ground.

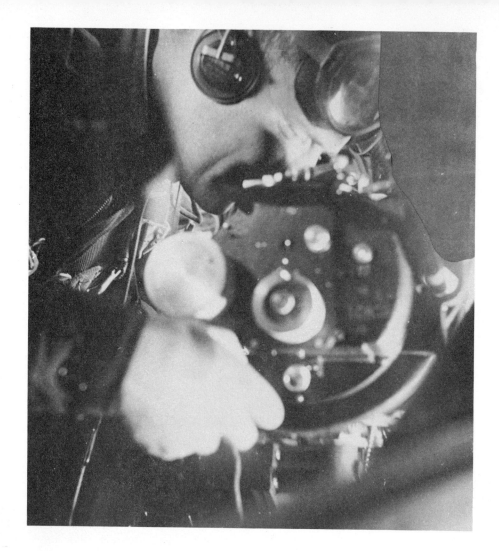

The man at left is about to squeeze a trigger which will send several hundred thousand tons of nuclear hell plunging through the air. An Air Force bombardier, he is sighting through a Norden bombsight while on an actual atomic bomb run at the Nevada Proving Ground. Tests of this nature are often held with Strategic Air Command bombers. Much of the rigorous SAC training program is incessant, competitive and exacting. Crews fly long, realistic missions to bomb simulated targets that have every possible resemblance to the actual targets they would be assigned if war plans were put into effect. The results in efficiency are unquestionable; "bombs on the target" by SAC crews is almost a foregone conclusion.

The stockpile of nuclear and thermonuclear weapons available to the strategic and tactical air commands endows the USAF with the explosive force to obliterate every possible target in the world. Nuclear weapons tests (*below:* the shot on March 22, 1955) have produced a family of atomic weapons which permit greater flexibility for the air strategy. These weapons range from atomic bombs of a size comparable to a portable typewriter, to thermonuclear arms which release several times the combined energy of all conventional bombs ever exploded.

"Biggest stick" of all—the B-52

When the Air Force made its decision a decade ago to order into production the Boeing B-52 Stratofortress bomber (*above:* they cost $8,000,000 each), it thereby decided in favor of a truly all-jet intercontinental strategic air force. In the years since World War II the USAF has laboriously built a large system of overseas air bases; using air tankers to extend their range, B-47s from these bases can reach any target in the Soviet Union. Since many of the fields are vulnerable to atomic attack, this arrangement at best is unsatisfactory. The delivery of the B-52 — capable of flight at altitudes well beyond 50,000 feet, with a top speed in the vicinity of 700 mph, carrying the most powerful bombs ever assembled, and using air-to-air refueling to extend its normal range of 6,000 miles — modified the structure of SAC in the direction of an intercontinental all-jet force. When B-52s have replaced the B-36 as our standard heavy bomber (a process now under way), the USAF will be able to launch a major nuclear assault with jet bombers in any direction, to any spot on the globe, from bases within the United States. Yet, even the massive B-52 is only another rung on the strategic-air-power ladder. When the first B-52A rolled off the production line, General Nathan Twining said, "Forget it. . . Start thinking about the next one, a bigger one, a faster one."

In nuclear weapons test, a SAC airman plots the bomb run of a jet bomber with its predicted course over Proving Ground.

Today the USAF's first-line day superiority fighter airplane, North American F-100 Sabre, ushered the USAF into the era of supersonic combat equipment. Able to reach speeds near 900 mph in the latest versions, the outstanding F-100 also boasts long range, heavy firepower, high fighting altitudes. There are fighter-bomber, escort versions.

The most heavy armed fighter in the world, Northrop F-89D Scorpion, carries 104 2.75-in. rockets, a two-man crew and elaborate radar equipment for all-weather and night interception missions. New F-89H is armed with both the 2.75-in. rockets and six GAR-1 Falcon guided missiles. With the Lockheed F-94C and North American F-86D, Scorpions provide air defense of U.S. New Convair F-102A is supersonic interceptor.

This man, standing his tour of duty as an aircraft spotter of the Ground Observers Corps, on a lonely tower on Vashon Island off Washington, is equally as essential to the air-defense system of the U.S. as a radar operator in a command center. Low-altitude gaps of radar leave big holes in air defense which can be filled only by visual observers.

Somewhere in the United States, at an Air Defense Command interceptor base, this scene is being repeated at this very moment. Jet fighter pilots remain on alert status, on order to scramble to intercept unidentifiable planes; can be airborne in storms or at night within two to four minutes after a warning.

A cure for insomnia

The massive airplane in the above picture is a late model of the Convair B-36, a ten-engined, 205-ton monster which to this day is the only airplane ever built capable of flying 10,000-mile intercontinental missions without aerial refueling. The development of the B-36 began in April of 1941; coming into service too late for the war, it was placed in the unenviable position of bridging the gap between wartime aircraft and the new generation of postwar jet bombers. Originally built with six piston engines, it was modified to add four jets to push its speed past 435 mph. Designed to carry up to 42 tons of conventional bombs, it was modified for nuclear, then thermonuclear weapons. It was designed in the maturity of one air age, and it flew in the infancy of another. As such, it inevitably became the stormy petrel of combat aviation. The record, however, should be kept clear. As the backbone of the Strategic Air Command during the crucial days of the cold war, the B-36 was the *only* weapon capable of destroying Russian cities in a sustained offensive. That this airplane never dropped a bomb in anger while passing on to obsolescence is only to its credit; it won the Cold War. The perfect weapon is the one you never have to use. And without the B-36, available as it was during a time of great national peril, the United States might have been forced to fight a disastrous air war of one-way missions.

This mechanic, making an adjustment in the air intake of two of the B-36D's ten engines, is working in 40-degrees-below-zero weather, during *Operation North Star* tests in Alaska in 1954 which used the giant bombers as simulated enemy raiders. Capable of flying 10,000 miles with a heavy bomb load, the latest B-36s constitute a first-line force for the Strategic Air Command. Special modifications carry jet fighters which can be launched in flight to hit enemy targets with atomic bombs, and are then retrieved. Other versions launch air-to-ground missiles for increased combat effectiveness; with its 16 cannon and other equipment removed, the B-36 flies at "unbelievable heights."

When the Air Force established 137 wings as the minimum needed for the nation's security, it did so with the knowledge that all the wings would have to be combat-ready. With weapons systems becoming increasingly complex and with new wings being formed at a time when the world situation would not allow the diminution of operational wings to provide cadres for the new units, the Air Training Command stepped into the breach by extending its training to include crew training. In contrast to the old system whereby a crewman received realistic combat training only after assignment to an operational unit, ATC now develops the combat-ready pilot or crew. ATC gained the responsibility of training not only new pilot-graduates, but of providing a transition period to adapt veteran pilots to new equipment *(above: checking out in new jet fighter)*. At Nellis AFB, where T-33s *(below)* are used for instrument work, flying activity is almost unbelievable. Jet fighters land or take off every 20 seconds of the day on the world's busiest field.

No other non-combat airplane has so changed military air operations in the postwar years as the deep-bellied Douglas C-124 Globemaster. An immense four-engine machine developed from the Douglas C-74, the Globemaster's ability to airlift cargoes up to thirty tons in weight, or as many as 200 fully equipped combat soldiers, made the years-old dream of air logistics a pleasant reality. The airplane's cavernous holds can do more than merely lift 60,000 pounds of cargo; giant clamshell nose doors and loading ramps allow tanks, trucks, other vehicles and cumbersome equipment to be airlifted in whole, rather than being broken down into many parts which must be reassembled in a battle area. In the Korean War, the Globemaster proved invaluable in transporting litter patients from the scene of battle to stateside hospitals. As an integral part of our global air forces, Globemaster units can airlift essential parts and men to any part of the world. Next in the Douglas line is the C-132—a 250-ton giant!

The power to lift mountains

The weird structure at left, belching forth brilliant flames and dense smoke clouds, is a rocket-test stand located high along a ridge in the Santa Susana Mountains in California. It is a difficult place to reach, and the narrow, winding road which leads to the Rocketdyne testing site of North American Aviation is impressively lined with armed guards. For Rocketdyne is the key to a fantastic future of intercontinental missiles and manned spaceships — both of which have advanced beyond the design stages. To see and hear one of these immense rocket motors is an incredible, mind-shattering experience. Men unprepared for the onslaught of the screaming thunder have literally lost control of their bodily functions. *(Below)* Within a thick concrete tunnel running beneath a missile-launching pad at Cape Canaveral, part of the Air Force Missile Test Center in Florida, a technician who has just armed an intercontinental missile completes an electronic circuit which will permit the weapon to be launched. Cape Canaveral is part of the USAF's quarter-billion-dollar missile-test facility.

Despite biased criticism from many quarters, the USAF guided missile program in most respects commands a leading superiority over the activities of the USSR and other nations. The Northrop SM-62 Snark (above), shown on its checkout and launching pad at Cape Canaveral, has been flying in tests for years. It is the world's first—and only successful—intercontinental-range missile. Capable of a 5,000-mile flight at high subsonic speeds, the Snark represents a tremendous technological break-through in missile design, leaping the gulf between a tactical weapon to a true strategic system.

Secluded within a thicket near the Iron Curtain in Germany, USAF crewmen of a pilotless bomber squadron carry out a simulated combat launching of the Martin TM-61A Matador (below), the USAF's first operational tactical missile. Capable of high subsonic speeds over an 800-mile range, the Matador can be launched under virtually any field conditions, in storms and at night, and with "astonishing accuracy." In mass production for several years, the Matador was accepted for operational service only after extensive tests proved the high accuracy of the missile.

The search without end

Within a Wright Air Development Center pressure chamber, a pilot watches water "explode," as would his blood at 70,000 feet.

The obstacles which man faces in his struggle to climb the vertical frontiers of flight are numerous, terrifying and easily fatal. The airman's newest machines are almost too much for the human mind and body; the experiences of everyday flight, not only at the experimental centers but at operational bases as well, daily subject pilots to a bewildering variety of forces which can explode a man's blood or smash his body to a pulp through severe acceleration and deceleration. There is a great meat grinder waiting in the sky for the unwary or the unprotected airman. The USAF for years has maintained elaborate laboratories in the air and on the ground to develop the equipment to keep its men alive and in fighting condition. Volunteers like the man on a rocket sled *(above)* are the pioneers of the vertical frontier, whose ultimate rewards point far beyond the sky.

Technicians wheel the sleek Bell X-2 rocket research plane toward its B-50 mother aircraft, which will carry the little sweptwing machine to 6 miles altitude, and then jettison it for its own powered flight. Embodying the latest developments in rocket power, aerodynamic design and instrumentation for advanced research, the X-2 has taken pilots through the air at better than 2,000 mph, and has soared to heights exceeding 126,000 feet. At this altitude above the earth a man literally is in open space. A pilot at this altitude, should his cabin pressure and suit fail, would find his body fluids bursting explosively *(center picture)*. USAF is now building the first manned spaceships.

NACA — the National Advisory Committee for Aeronautics — has sometimes been referred to as the greatest aeronautical brain center in the world. The description is an accurate one. Some 7,500 people work in three large research centers and two field stations to solve the most pressing problems in aircraft design and development, as well as to chart a path for the future through pure aeronautical research. If any one organization can be considered indispensable to our air progress, it clearly is NACA.

"Put out my hand and touched the face of God."

When we are done with it — the screaming jets and their afterburners, the ungodly thunder of the great rockets, the leviathans which beat the air with their mighty wings; when we sum up all the tools of this new air age — the banks of gleaming tubes, the fine imprints of transistors, the glowing radar panels and scopes; when we total the massive organization needed to support our airpower; when we note the charts and graphs with their statistics of bomb tonnages and millions of gallons of fuel; all this — and the engineers' dreams with their slide rules, the excited talk of hypersonic flight where the blue of earth's sky dissolves into blackness — it is as nothing without the most essential ingredient of all . . . man's love of flying. There are no precision instruments to measure what a pilot finds with his heart and his mind in the "high untrespassed sanctity of space." We cannot capture with our inadequate words the infinite freedom and sparkling joyousness of the airman's world. But it is there, it belongs to these men who fly. Without this fierce longing, without this sense of freedom in the high, unbounded blue, without the flier to breathe life into the inert, winged machines — man would still be chained to the ground.

Pilot Officer John G. Magee, Jr.

The pictures used in this book are from the United States Air Force, with the following exceptions: pages 3 (upper left), 8 (upper left), and page 12 are from the Institute of the Aeronautical Sciences; pages 10, 11 (lower right), and 63 are from Underwood & Underwood; pages 16, 17 (bottom), 23 (upper left), 24 (lower left), and 25 are from the Peter M. Bowers Collection; pages 19 (upper right), 21 (lower left), and 23 (bottom) are from The National Archives; pages 77 (bottom) and 80 (top) are from the David C. Cooke Collection; pages 80 (bottom), 91 (top) and 126 are from Lockheed Aircraft Corporation; pages 81 (middle), 90 (bottom), 96 (bottom), 139 (bottom), 205 (top), and 228 (bottom) are from Bell Aircraft Corporation; page 84 from the United States Signal Corps; pages 110 (top), 111 (bottom), 113, 124 (upper right and bottom) and 125 (top) are from the United States Army; pages 200 (bottom), 204 (top), 214 and 219 (top) are from Boeing Airplane Company; page 201 (bottom) is from Northrop Aircraft, Inc.; pages 205 (bottom) and 227 (bottom) are from The Glenn L. Martin Company; pages 220 and 226 (top) are from North American Aviation, Inc.; page 222 is from Convair; and page 229 from the National Advisory Committee for Aeronautics.